This book belongs to

_____

Anchor Me

Anchor Me

Laying a Foundation in Bible Study and Prayer
(Devotional)

Patti Greene

WESTBOW
PRESS®
A DIVISION OF THOMAS NELSON
& ZONDERVAN

Unless otherwise indicated, all Scripture quotations are taken from the Holy Bible, New Living Translation, copyright ©1996, 2004, 2007 by Tyndale House Foundation. Used by Permission of Tyndale House Publishers, Inc., Carol Stream, Illinois 60188. All rights reserved.

WestBow Press books may be ordered through booksellers or by contacting:

WestBow Press
A Division of Thomas Nelson & Zondervan
1663 Liberty Drive
Bloomington, IN 47403
www.westbowpress.com
1 (866) 928-1240

ISBN: 978-1-4908-9317-4 (sc)
ISBN: 978-1-4908-9531-4 (e)

Print information available on the last page.

WestBow Press rev. date: 02/02/2016

Dedicated to My Nigerian Friends
Ann, Asabe, Glory, Lucky, and Titi

If a ship is not secured to a strong anchor,
it is left to the mercy of the winds and currents.
The ship would drift hopelessly
in no particular direction.

A.B., Ship Captain

Acknowledgments

I first want to thank the Lord for giving me the inspiration and the stick-to-itiveness to complete this project. It was not my intent to write my words in this book. My intention was to write a devotional prayer journal with guidance from the Holy Spirit.

I thank my husband, John, my children, and my parents for always believing in me and praying for me even when my ideas seem outrageous or unreachable.

I also want to thank Pippa Fields and Kristy Davis who spent valuable time sharing suggestions as I narrowed down these topics. Their skills in counseling and education respectively helped me conceptualize both the topics and page design of this book.

Appreciation and thanks go to my friend and writer, Glory C. Odemene, who graciously offered her gift of poetry through enlightening excerpts scattered throughout the book.

I wish to thank inkprince.com for their technical expertise and artistic talent in creating a gorgeous cover for *Anchor Me: Laying a Foundation in Bible Study and Prayer*. I love the cover more and more every day.

Additional thanks to copy-editor Kristy Davis. Not only did she meticulously pore over the spelling, grammar, and punctuation of the book, but she also evaluated the structure of the raw manuscript making this book more readable to its audience.

Patti Greene

Table of Contents

List of Illustrations

Preface

Hebrews 6:18-19 states, "So God has given both his promise and his oath. These two things are unchangeable because it is impossible for God to lie. Therefore, we who have fled to Him for refuge can have great confidence as we hold to the hope that lies before us. This hope is a strong and trustworthy **ANCHOR** for our souls. It leads us through the curtain into God's inner sanctuary." This verse is saying that when we hope in God and trust His promises we can be anchored in our souls and be lead into a deeper walk with Him. Right where you are—in your home, in your school, at your job, and in your church, people are watching to see who you are anchored to, what rules you abide by, what interests you have, and how your life is different from theirs. God believes in your potential. I see this same potential in you, and that is why I have written this book, *Anchor Me: Laying a Foundation in Bible Study and Prayer*.

I personally made a commitment to follow Christ during my teenage years. Many God-fearing adults graciously trained me to become the person God intended me to be. Now, with some experience and growth behind me, it is my turn and desire to help you develop a deeper walk with the Lord.

I was privileged to be able to work with young adults on a daily basis during a major portion of my adult life. For fifteen years, I worked as a high school librarian. It was there I encountered secondary students from all walks of life. I gleaned many insights into the pressures students face by observing and interacting with them daily. Every student I encountered was unique. They all had challenges unique to them, as well as common challenges that affected all students every day whether it was studying for exams, dealing with an unreasonable teacher, trying out for a sports team, or even being in the midst of a cafeteria food fight. Through the years, I shared their ups and downs, successes and failures, heartthrobs and heartaches, and as a result many of my students made their way into my daily prayer journal. What a privilege and a joy it was to be able to pray for them!

My desire is for you to recognize that God has given you the same privilege to pray for others and yourself. *Anchor Me* is a 181-day, undated, "issue-based" journal designed just for you – a busy person – to track your life story and to help you learn the benefits of walking the Christian walk through daily Bible study and prayer. Contemporary issues such as faith, love, depression, drug addiction, stress, and self-image are covered Biblically to give you the strength and courage you need to face each day. So, grab a pen, a Bible, and spend a few minutes each day focusing on God, the Bible, and prayer.

Keeping track of my prayers (also known as prayer journaling) has been part of my life since I was a young adult. I was prayer journaling before "prayer journaling" was even part of Christian terminology. I can look back now at my journals (yes, I still have them) and I am amazed at some of the requests I formerly had and how God answered them. I prayed for a particular boy to become my husband, but He gave me one much better. I prayed I would pass my college criminology test, and I did. I prayed for the right classes and teachers, and He chose the teachers that were best for me. My life story is written into the pages of my forty-three annual journals. God knows your life story. He knows the big picture of your life. I hope, as you work through this book, through Bible study and prayer, that the Lord's love and blessings will keep you strong and in love with Jesus Christ.

This devotional is ideal for individual use, prayer groups, Bible study groups, family study groups, or during any free time you might have. A Leader/Facilitator guide is included at the back of the book for those desiring to make this devotional a group learning experience. It includes general meeting tips for the leader and facilitator to use at their introductory, before, during, and after sessions.

As a final word to all growing believers using this devotional, I applaud you for your desire to grow by being involved in Bible study and prayer. May you never forget that God always has your best interests in mind. He loves you with an everlasting love. His Word, the Bible, has much to say about how you should live your life. Embrace His Word. Let His words penetrate deep down into your soul. May your desire to obey the Lord intensify as you seek Him. Let Bible study and prayer become your guide during this exciting time in your life.

Introduction

"Lord, I am so lonely. I wish I had just one friend."
"I can't take it if my boss doesn't appreciate all
the work I have done AGAIN!"
"If that teacher yells at me today, I don't know how I will react."

Do you find yourself needing a little inspiration to get through your daily life and routine? Anchor *Me* is a 181-day, undated, devotional prayer journal designed purposely to help you become stronger about Biblical topics you might encounter any day of the week. God's love and mercies are always available to you. This devotional gives you a few moments to think about what God says, to think about your day, and to plan your day through prayer. And, it can be started at any day of the year for your convenience!

There is no right or wrong way to use *Anchor Me*. Just allow your thoughts and prayers to flow freely onto the pages. You can work in this journal from the front to the back, from the back to the front, from topic to topic of interest to you, or by the "open up the book and point randomly" method. By using the index in the back of the book, you will find a wonderful way to see all the topics and page numbers at a glance.

The entries in this journal consist of the following:

1. A dateline
2. A topic of interest
3. A corresponding Bible verse
4. A suggested chapter reading from either Psalms or Proverbs
5. A "What does the Bible verse or Bible chapter mean to you?" section
6. A thought provoking question for you to answer
7. An area to write prayers requests and notes
8. A "What is God teaching you or asking you to do?" section

The dateline on each page is intentionally left blank, because I do not want you to ever feel guilty if you miss a day. The goal is to use this book as a guide on as many days as possible, but sometimes that just doesn't happen. You will get busy with homework, projects, sports, music, and much more. So if you miss a day, just pick up where you left off and keep going.

As I wrote this book, my goal was to create a "no pressure guide" to help you in your daily devotionals and to nurture a love for the Word of God. On each page, whether you decide to have a long reflection time or a quick go-through, any time spent in God's Word and in prayer will be beneficial in your walk with the Lord.

When you complete this book, you will have read the entire book Psalms and Proverbs. Hiding the Word of God in your heart each day will build a stronger relationship with the Lord. The Lord will show you His desires for your life as you consistently lean on His Word for guidance.

Here are a few suggestions:

1. Keep this devotional by your bed and work on it daily—preferably in the morning before your day starts.
2. If you bring it to school or work with you, keep it in your backpack or bag. Don't leave it in your locker or your car; it may just get lost in the shuffle.
3. Consider keeping your devotional with you wherever you go. You never know when you will feel the need to focus on God. But be careful not to lose it! You may end up writing some personal notes in it that you would not want anyone else to see.
4. Buy one for your best friend or mentee and go through it together. You can share what your thoughts and prayers are for the day over lunch or free time. Sharing together is one way to grow and become accountable in your Christian walk. Besides, your Christian friendships may be exactly what both you and they need to help face daily challenges and situations.
5. Try using this book at the same time every day to develop consistency in your journey.

6. Share the daily verse with those you know. Post it on your social media sites and get some conversations flowing!
7. Keep this devotional FOREVER. You will love looking back on it years from now to see how God answered your prayers! You will be amazed at how far you've come!

With much prayer and joy, I invite you to join me in the quest for a deeper walk with the Lord. Please feel free to contact me to share what God is doing in your life and how this book has helped you.

In addition, I would greatly appreciate it if you would take a little bit of your time to leave a review on Amazon, Barnes and Noble, or any review site. Reviews are hard to get, but it helps so much in getting the word out to potential readers who may desire to learn more about the foundations in Bible study and prayer. I would also be honored if you would join my social media sites. They are located on my website at www.PattiGreene.com. Thank you.

Patti Greene, Author of *Anchor Me: Laying a Foundation in Bible Study and Prayer.*

Other Books by Author: *Awaken Me: Growing Deeper in Bible Study and Prayer*

Books of the Bible

The Old Testament

Genesis	2 Chronicles	Daniel
Exodus	Ezra	Hosea
Leviticus	Nehemiah	Joel
Numbers	Esther	Amos
Deuteronomy	Job	Obadiah
Joshua	Psalms	Jonah
Judges	Proverbs	Micah
Ruth	Ecclesiastes	Nahum
1 Samuel	Song of Songs	Habakkuk
2 Samuel	Isaiah	Zephaniah
1 Kings	Jeremiah	Haggai
2 Kings	Lamentations	Zechariah
1 Chronicles	Ezekiel	Malachi

The New Testament

Matthew	Ephesians	Hebrews
Mark	Philippians	James
Luke	Colossians	1 Peter
John	1 Thessalonians	2 Peter
Acts	2 Thessalonians	1 John
Romans	1 Timothy	2 John
1 Corinthians	2 Timothy	3 John
2 Corinthians	Titus	Jude
Galatians	Philemon	Revelation

It's Work

Business People Working

So I labor to focus all I presently possess
To learn the rules and run circumspectly
The race set before me, in pursuit of what
I desire tomorrow, knowing there is neither
Limit not end to rewards and gratifications
That awaits those who train and run to win.

Poetry Credit: *The Race*, Glory
C. Odemene ©2013

Date: _____

Athletics and Contests

Don't you realize that in a race everyone runs, but only one person
gets the prize? So run to win! All athletes are disciplined in their
training. They do it to win a prize that will fade away, but we do
it for an eternal prize. So I run with purpose in every step.
I am not just shadowboxing.

(1 Corinthians 9:24-26; Read Psalm 1)

✝✝

What does the Bible verse or Bible chapter mean to you?

_____

_____

Why do some people feel the need to cheat in competitions?

_____

_____

List your PRAYER REQUESTS and PRAY.

☐ _____

☐ _____

☐ _____

☐ _____

What is God teaching you or asking you to do?

_____

_____

Date: _____

Bad Company

Don't be fooled by those who say such things,
for "bad company corrupts good character."

(1 Corinthians 15:33; Read Psalm 2)

✝✝

What does the Bible verse or Bible chapter mean to you?

_____

_____

How do you recognize good company from bad company?

_____

_____

List your PRAYER REQUESTS and PRAY.

☐ _____

☐ _____

☐ _____

☐ _____

What is God teaching you or asking you to do?

_____

_____

Date: _____

Boredom / Idleness

Plant your seed in the morning and keep busy all afternoon, for you don't know if profit will come from one activity or another —or maybe both.

(Ecclesiastes 11:6; Read Psalm 3)

††

What does the Bible verse or Bible chapter mean to you?

_____

_____

Why do we get bored sometimes?

_____

_____

List your PRAYER REQUESTS and PRAY.

☐ _____

☐ _____

☐ _____

☐ _____

What is God teaching you or asking you to do?

_____

_____

Date: _____

Cheating

If you are faithful in little things, you will be faithful in large ones.
But if you are dishonest in little things,
you won't be honest with greater responsibilities.

(Luke 16:10; Read Psalm 4)

✝✝

What does the Bible verse or Bible chapter mean to you?

_____

_____

Why do students feel pressure or temptation to cheat?

_____

_____

List your PRAYER REQUESTS and PRAY.

☐ _____

☐ _____

☐ _____

☐ _____

What is God teaching you or asking you to do?

_____

_____

Date: _____

Competitiveness

Pay careful attention to your own work,
for then you will get the satisfaction of a job well done,
and you won't need to compare yourself to anyone else.
For we are each responsible for our own conduct.

(Galatians 6:4-5; Read Psalm 5)

†††

What does the Bible verse or Bible chapter mean to you?

_____

_____

How can competitiveness lead us to do wrong sometime? Explain.

_____

_____

List your PRAYER REQUESTS and PRAY.

☐ _____

☐ _____

☐ _____

☐ _____

What is God teaching you or asking you to do?

_____

_____

Date: _____

Disabilities / Uniqueness

God works in different ways, but it is the same
God who does the work in all of us.

(1 Corinthians 12:6; Read Psalm 6)

††

What does the Bible verse or Bible chapter mean to you?

_____

_____

How can we accept one another despite our differences?

_____

_____

List your PRAYER REQUESTS and PRAY.

☐ _____

☐ _____

☐ _____

☐ _____

What is God teaching you or asking you to do?

_____

_____

Date: _____

Failure

Then David continued, "Be strong and courageous, and do the work.
Don't be afraid or discouraged, for the LORD God, my God, is with
you. He will not fail you or forsake you. He will see to it that all the
work related to the Temple of the LORD is finished correctly."

(1 Chronicles 28:20; Read Psalm 7)

††

What does the Bible verse or Bible chapter mean to you?

_____

_____

Why is it important never to give up?

_____

_____

List your PRAYER REQUESTS and PRAY.

☐ _____

☐ _____

☐ _____

☐ _____

What is God teaching you or asking you to do?

_____

_____

Date: _____

Fighting

Starting a quarrel is like opening a floodgate,
so stop before a dispute breaks out.

(Proverbs 17:14; Read Psalm 8)

†††

What does the Bible verse or Bible chapter mean to you?

_____

_____

Why is starting a fight an unwise thing to do?

_____

_____

List your PRAYER REQUESTS and PRAY.

- ☐ _____
- ☐ _____
- ☐ _____
- ☐ _____

What is God teaching you or asking you to do?

_____

_____

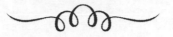

Date: _____

Friendship

A friend is always loyal,
and a brother is born to help in time of need.

(Proverbs 17:17; Read Psalm 9)

✝✝

What does the Bible verse or Bible chapter mean to you?

_____

_____

Define <u>friendship</u> in your own words.

_____

_____

List your PRAYER REQUESTS and PRAY.

☐ _____

☐ _____

☐ _____

☐ _____

What is God teaching you or asking you to do?

_____

_____

Date: _____

Generosity

But generous people plan to do what is generous,
and they stand firm in their generosity.

(Isaiah 32:8; Read Psalm 10)

††

What does the Bible verse or Bible chapter mean to you?

_____

_____

How can you show generosity to your co-workers or classmates?

_____

_____

List your PRAYER REQUESTS and PRAY.

☐ _____

☐ _____

☐ _____

☐ _____

What is God teaching you or asking you to do?

_____

_____

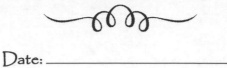

Date: _____

Goals

Mark out a straight path for your feet so that those who are
weak and lame will not fall but become strong.

(Hebrews 12:13; Read Psalm 11)

††

What does the Bible verse or Bible chapter mean to you?

_____

_____

Describe a time you gave yourself wholeheartedly to a goal.

_____

_____

List your PRAYER REQUESTS and PRAY.

☐ _____

☐ _____

☐ _____

☐ _____

What is God teaching you or asking you to do?

_____

_____

Date: _____

Guidance

Let the wise listen to these proverbs and become even wiser.
Let those with understanding receive guidance.

(Proverbs 1:5; Read Psalm 12)

††

What does the Bible verse or Bible chapter mean to you?

_____

_____

What could happen to us if we do not accept wise guidance?

_____

_____

List your PRAYER REQUESTS and PRAY.

☐ _____

☐ _____

☐ _____

☐ _____

What is God teaching you or asking you to do?

_____

_____

Date: _____

Knowledge and Learning

I believe in your commands;
now teach me good judgment and knowledge.
I used to wander off until you disciplined me;
but now I closely follow your word.
You are good and do only good; teach me your decrees.

(Psalm 119:66-68; Read Psalm 13)

††

What does the Bible verse or Bible chapter mean to you?

_____

_____

How do you measure your success in school or at work?

_____

_____

List your PRAYER REQUESTS and PRAY.

☐ _____

☐ _____

☐ _____

☐ _____

What is God teaching you or asking you to do?

_____

_____

Date: _____

Laziness

Lazy people want much but get little, but
those who work hard will prosper.

(Proverbs 13:4; Read Psalm 14)

††

What does the Bible verse or Bible chapter mean to you?

_____

_____

Why does God want us to be productive?

_____

_____

List your PRAYER REQUESTS and PRAY.

- ☐ _____
- ☐ _____
- ☐ _____
- ☐ _____

What is God teaching you or asking you to do?

_____

_____

Date: _____

Loneliness

Turn to me and have mercy, for
I am alone and in deep distress.

(Psalm 25:16; Read Psalm 15)

††

What does the Bible verse or Bible chapter mean to you?

_____

_____

What can you do to help someone who is lonely?

_____

_____

List your PRAYER REQUESTS and PRAY.

☐ _____

☐ _____

☐ _____

☐ _____

What is God teaching you or asking you to do?

_____

_____

Date: _____

Materialism

Then he said, "Beware! Guard against every kind of greed.
Life is not measured by how much you own.

(Luke 12:15; Read Psalm 16)

✝✝✝

What does the Bible verse or Bible chapter mean to you?

_____

_____

How can you guard against loving your possessions?

_____

_____

List your PRAYER REQUESTS and PRAY.

☐ _____

☐ _____

☐ _____

☐ _____

What is God teaching you or asking you to do?

_____

_____

Date: _____

Perfectionism

Each time [The Lord] said, "My grace is all you need.
My power works best in weakness." So now I am glad to boast about
my weaknesses, so that the power of Christ can work through me."

(2 Corinthians 12:9; Read Psalm 17)

††
What does the Bible verse or Bible chapter mean to you?

_____

_____

Have you ever tried to be perfect at something? Did it work out?

_____

_____

List your PRAYER REQUESTS and PRAY.

☐ _____

☐ _____

☐ _____

☐ _____

What is God teaching you or asking you to do?

_____

_____

Date: _____

Popularity

Obviously, I'm not trying to win the approval of people, but of God.
If pleasing people were my goal, I would not be Christ's servant.

(Galatians 1:10; Read Psalm 18)

††
What does the Bible verse or Bible chapter mean to you?

_____

_____

Why is being popular so important to some people?

_____

_____

List your PRAYER REQUESTS and PRAY.

☐ _____

☐ _____

☐ _____

☐ _____

What is God teaching you or asking you to do?

_____

_____

Date: _____

Priorities

Trust in the LORD with all your heart;
do not depend on your own understanding.
Seek his will in all you do,
and he will show you which path to take.

(Proverbs 3:5-6; Read Psalm 19)

††

What does the Bible verse or Bible chapter mean to you?

_____

_____

What are your 2 main priorities at this moment in your life?

_____

_____

List your PRAYER REQUESTS and PRAY.

☐ _____

☐ _____

☐ _____

☐ _____

What is God teaching you or asking you to do?

_____

_____

Date: _____

Procrastination

A little extra sleep, a little more slumber,
a little folding of the hands to rest—
then poverty will pounce on you like a bandit;
scarcity will attack you like an armed robber.

(Proverbs 6:10-11; Read Psalm 20)

††

What does the Bible verse or Bible chapter mean to you?

_____

_____

Are you a procrastinator? What do you tend to put off?

_____

_____

List your PRAYER REQUESTS and PRAY.

☐ _____

☐ _____

☐ _____

☐ _____

What is God teaching you or asking you to do?

_____

_____

Date: _____

Profanity

Don't use foul or abusive language.
Let everything you say be good and helpful, so
that your words will be an encouragement to those who hear them.

(Ephesians 4:29; Read Psalm 21)

††

What does the Bible verse or Bible chapter mean to you?

_____

_____

How can you keep yourself from swearing?

_____

_____

List your PRAYER REQUESTS and PRAY.

☐ _____

☐ _____

☐ _____

☐ _____

What is God teaching you or asking you to do?

_____

_____

Date: _____

Quitting

So let's not get tired of doing what is good. At just the right time
we will reap a harvest of blessing if we don't give up.

(Galatians 6:9; Read Psalm 22)

✝✝✝

What does the Bible verse or Bible chapter mean to you?

_____

_____

Why are people so quick to quit, i.e. school, job, marriage?

_____

_____

List your PRAYER REQUESTS and PRAY.

☐ _____

☐ _____

☐ _____

☐ _____

What is God teaching you or asking you to do?

_____

_____

Date: _____

Reputation

Choose a good reputation over great riches;
being held in high esteem is better than silver or gold.

(Proverbs 22:1; Read Psalm 23)

††

What does the Bible verse or Bible chapter mean to you?

_____

_____

Why is having a Godly reputation important?

_____

_____

List your PRAYER REQUESTS and PRAY.

☐ _____

☐ _____

☐ _____

☐ _____

What is God teaching you or asking you to do?

_____

_____

Date: _____

Respecting Teachers and Bosses

Everyone must submit to governing authorities.
For all authority comes from God, and those
in positions of authority have been placed there by God.

(Romans 13:1; Read Psalm 24)

†††

What does the Bible verse or Bible chapter mean to you?

_____

_____

Why are some teachers and bosses easier to respect than others?

_____

_____

List your PRAYER REQUESTS and PRAY.

☐ _____

☐ _____

☐ _____

☐ _____

What is God teaching you or asking you to do?

_____

_____

Date: _____

Success

Jesus replied, "You must love the LORD your God with
all your heart, all your soul, and all your mind.
This is the first and greatest commandment."

(Matthew 22:37-38; Read Psalm 25)

††

What does the Bible verse or Bible chapter mean to you?

_____

_____

Name one area you would like to be successful in. Why?

_____

_____

List your PRAYER REQUESTS and PRAY.

☐ _____

☐ _____

☐ _____

☐ _____

What is God teaching you or asking you to do?

_____

_____

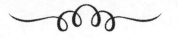

Date: _____

Work

Even while we were with you, we gave you this command:
"Those unwilling to work will not get to eat."

(2 Thessalonians 3:10; Read Psalm 26)

††

What does the Bible verse or Bible chapter mean to you?

_____

_____

What does the quality of your work reveal about you?

_____

_____

List your PRAYER REQUESTS and PRAY.

☐ _____

☐ _____

☐ _____

☐ _____

What is God teaching you or asking you to do?

_____

_____

Date: _____

Your Conversation

Live wisely among those who are not believers,
and make the most of every opportunity.
Let your conversation be gracious and attractive so that
you will have the right response for everyone.

(Colossians 4:5-6; Read Psalm 27)

✝✝✝

What does the Bible verse or Bible chapter mean to you?

_____

_____

Recall a situation where you said something you shouldn't have.

_____

_____

List your PRAYER REQUESTS and PRAY.

☐ _____

☐ _____

☐ _____

☐ _____

What is God teaching you or asking you to do?

_____

_____

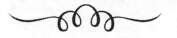

Date: _____

Youth

Don't let anyone think less of you because you are young.
Be an example to all believers in what you say, in the way you live,
in your love, your faith, and your purity.

(1Timothy 4:12; Read Psalm 28)

††

What does the Bible verse or Bible chapter mean to you?

_____

_____

What are some ways you can make a positive difference for Christ?

_____

_____

List your PRAYER REQUESTS and PRAY.

☐ _____

☐ _____

☐ _____

☐ _____

What is God teaching you or asking you to do?

_____

_____

It's Emotional

Sad Young Fellow

"Despite everyday riddles that baffle us
Life reserves the finest for the persistent:
Keep your eyes straight, your heart light
And till you get there, don't give up!"

Poetry Credit: *Don't Give Up,*
Glory C. Odemene ©2014

Date: _____

Anger / Temper

Stop being angry!
Turn from your rage!
Do not lose your temper—
it only leads to harm.

(Psalm 37:8; Read Psalm 29)

††

What does the Bible verse or Bible chapter mean to you?

_____

_____

Recall a time you were angry.

_____

_____

List your PRAYER REQUESTS and PRAY.

☐ _____

☐ _____

☐ _____

☐ _____

What is God teaching you or asking you to do?

_____

_____

Date: _____

Anxiety

Give all your worries and cares to God, for he cares about you.

(1 Peter 5:7; Read Psalm 30)

††

What does the Bible verse or Bible chapter mean to you?

_____

_____

Describe the last time you were anxious about something.

_____

_____

List your PRAYER REQUESTS and PRAY.

☐ _____

☐ _____

☐ _____

☐ _____

What is God teaching you or asking you to do?

_____

_____

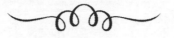

Date: _____

Arrogance

Don't think you are better than you really are.
Be honest in your evaluation of yourselves,
measuring yourselves by the faith God has given us.

(Romans 12:3b; Read Psalm 31)

✝✝

What does the Bible verse or Bible chapter mean to you?

_____

_____

What is the difference between being arrogant and being humble?

_____

_____

List your PRAYER REQUESTS and PRAY.

☐ _____

☐ _____

☐ _____

☐ _____

What is God teaching you or asking you to do?

_____

_____

Date: _____

Bitterness

Look after each other so that none of you fails to receive the
grace of God. Watch out that no poisonous root of bitterness
grows up to trouble you, corrupting many.

(Hebrews 12:15; Read Psalm 32)

✝✝✝

What does the Bible verse or Bible chapter mean to you?

_____

_____

How does bitterness take hold in someone's life?

_____

_____

List your PRAYER REQUESTS and PRAY.

☐ _____

☐ _____

☐ _____

☐ _____

What is God teaching you or asking you to do?

_____

_____

Date: _____

Brokenhearted

The LORD is close to the brokenhearted;
he rescues those whose spirits are crushed.

(Psalm 34:18; Read Psalm 33)

††

What does the Bible verse or Bible chapter mean to you?

_____

_____

Have you ever experienced a broken heart? Describe it.

_____

_____

List your PRAYER REQUESTS and PRAY.

☐ _____

☐ _____

☐ _____

☐ _____

What is God teaching you or asking you to do?

_____

_____

Date: _____

Confusion

Are you also confused? Is our champion helpless to save us?
You are right here among us, LORD.
We are known as your people. Please don't abandon us now!

(Jeremiah 14:9; Read Psalm 34)

††

What does the Bible verse or Bible chapter mean to you?

_____

_____

Describe a situation that was confusing and disorganized.

_____

_____

List your PRAYER REQUESTS and PRAY.

☐ _____

☐ _____

☐ _____

☐ _____

What is God teaching you or asking you to do?

_____

_____

Date: _____

Depression

"For I know the plans I have for you, says the LORD. They are plans for good and not for disaster, to give you a future and a hope."

(Jeremiah 29:11; Read Psalm 35)

✝✝

What does the Bible verse or Bible chapter mean to you?

_____

_____

What are the symptoms of depression?

_____

_____

List your PRAYER REQUESTS and PRAY.

☐ _____

☐ _____

☐ _____

☐ _____

What is God teaching you or asking you to do?

_____

_____

Date: _____

Discouragement

Why am I discouraged? Why is my heart so sad?
I will put my hope in God! I will praise him again—
my Savior and my God!

(Psalm 42:11; Read Psalm 36)

††

What does the Bible verse or Bible chapter mean to you?

_____

_____

What should you do when you are discouraged? See the verse above.

_____

_____

List your PRAYER REQUESTS and PRAY.

☐ _____

☐ _____

☐ _____

☐ _____

What is God teaching you or asking you to do?

_____

_____

Date: _____

Envy

For wherever there is jealousy and selfish ambition,
there you will find disorder and evil of every kind.

(James 3:16; Read Psalm 37)

†††

What does the Bible verse or Bible chapter mean to you?

_____

_____

Why is envy bad?

_____

_____

List your PRAYER REQUESTS and PRAY.

☐ _____

☐ _____

☐ _____

☐ _____

What is God teaching you or asking you to do?

_____

_____

Date: _____

Fear

The LORD is my light and my salvation—
so why should I be afraid?
The LORD is my fortress, protecting me from danger,
so why should I tremble?

(Psalm 27:1; Read Psalm 38)

††

What does the Bible verse or Bible chapter mean to you?

_____
_____

Name some fears you have experienced in your life.

_____
_____

List your PRAYER REQUESTS and PRAY.

☐ _____
☐ _____
☐ _____
☐ _____

What is God teaching you or asking you to do?

_____
_____

Date: _____

Fear of Others

For God has not given us a spirit of fear and timidity,
but of power, love, and self-discipline.

(2 Timothy 1:7; Read Psalm 39)

††

What does the Bible verse or Bible chapter mean to you?

_____

_____

Are you afraid around people? How you can overcome those fears?

_____

_____

List your PRAYER REQUESTS and PRAY.

- ☐ _____
- ☐ _____
- ☐ _____
- ☐ _____

What is God teaching you or asking you to do?

_____

_____

Date: _____

Grief

We hear songs of praise from the ends of the earth,
songs that give glory to the Righteous One!
But my heart is heavy with grief. Weep for me, for I wither away.
Deceit still prevails and treachery is everywhere.

(Isaiah 24:16; Read Psalm 40)

††

What does the Bible verse or Bible chapter mean to you?

_____

_____

What is the most important thing a grieving person needs?

_____

_____

List your PRAYER REQUESTS and PRAY.

☐ _____

☐ _____

☐ _____

☐ _____

What is God teaching you or asking you to do?

_____

_____

Date: _____

Hatred

Hatred stirs up quarrels,
but love makes up for all offenses.

(Proverbs 10:12; Read Psalm 41)

††

What does the Bible verse or Bible chapter mean to you?

_____

_____

How does God want you to deal with hatred?

_____

_____

List your PRAYER REQUESTS and PRAY.

☐ _____

☐ _____

☐ _____

☐ _____

What is God teaching you or asking you to do?

_____

_____

Date: _____

Hopelessness

I pray that God, the source of hope, will fill you completely with joy and peace because you trust in him. Then you will overflow with confident hope through the power of the Holy Spirit.

(Romans 15:13 Read Psalm 42)

✝✝

What does the Bible verse or Bible chapter mean to you?

_____

_____

Where does real hope come from?

_____

_____

List your PRAYER REQUESTS and PRAY.

☐ _____

☐ _____

☐ _____

☐ _____

What is God teaching you or asking you to do?

_____

_____

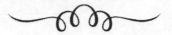

Date: _____

Inferiority Complex

But he said to me, "My grace is sufficient for you,
For my power is made perfect in weakness.

(2 Corinthians 12:9a; Read Psalm 43)

†††

What does the Bible verse or Bible chapter mean to you?

_____

_____

What experiences cause you to feel insecure and inferior?

_____

_____

List your PRAYER REQUESTS and PRAY.

☐ _____

☐ _____

☐ _____

☐ _____

What is God teaching you or asking you to do?

_____

_____

Date: _____

Jealousy

A peaceful heart leads to a healthy body;
jealousy is like cancer in the bones.

(Proverbs 14:30; Read Psalm 44)

✝✝

What does the Bible verse or Bible chapter mean to you?

_____

_____

What people or situations cause you to become jealous? Why?

_____

_____

List your PRAYER REQUESTS and PRAY.

☐ _____

☐ _____

☐ _____

☐ _____

What is God teaching you or asking you to do?

_____

_____

Date: _____

Rejection

You are coming to Christ, who is the living cornerstone
of God's temple. He was rejected by people, but
he was chosen by God for great honor.

(1 Peter 2:4; Read Psalm 45)

✝✝

What does the Bible verse or Bible chapter mean to you?

_____

_____

When someone rejects you, how should you deal with them?

_____

_____

List your PRAYER REQUESTS and PRAY.

☐ _____

☐ _____

☐ _____

☐ _____

What is God teaching you or asking you to do?

_____

_____

Date: _____

Stress

Even youths will become weak and tired, and young men will fall in
exhaustion. But those who trust in the LORD will find new strength.
They will soar high on wings like eagles.
They will run and not grow weary. They will walk and not faint.

(Isaiah 40:30-31; Read Psalm 46)

††

What does the Bible verse or Bible chapter mean to you?

_____

_____

Describe a time you were stressed out and how you handled it.

_____

_____

List your PRAYER REQUESTS and PRAY.

☐ _____

☐ _____

☐ _____

☐ _____

What is God teaching you or asking you to do?

_____

_____

Date: _____

Worry

That is why I tell you not to worry about everyday life—whether you have enough food and drink, or enough clothes to wear. Isn't life more than food, and your body more than clothing?
Seek the Kingdom of God above all else, and live righteously, and he will give you everything you need.

(Matthew 6:25, 33; Read Psalm 47)

††

What does the Bible verse or Bible chapter mean to you?

_____

_____

List the worries you are facing today.

_____

_____

List your PRAYER REQUESTS and PRAY.

☐ _____

☐ _____

☐ _____

☐ _____

What is God teaching you or asking you to do?

_____

_____

It's Tough

Homeless Girl counting Money

He said, "You are neither a
mistake nor a misfit
You're unique, like no other, and as you let Me
I will use you according to
your designed purpose."

Poetry Credit: *Cracks*, Glory
C. Odemene ©2013

Date: _____

Been Wronged?

Jesus said, "If another believer sins against you,
go privately and point out the offense. If the other person
listens and confesses it, you have won that person back."

(Matthew 18:15; Read Psalm 48)

††

What does the Bible verse or Bible chapter mean to you?

_____

_____

How do you feel when you are blamed for something you didn't do?

_____

_____

List your PRAYER REQUESTS and PRAY.

☐ _____

☐ _____

☐ _____

☐ _____

What is God teaching you or asking you to do?

_____

_____

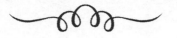

Date: _____

Complaining Spirit

Do everything without complaining and arguing, so that no one can criticize you. Live clean, innocent lives as children of God, shining like bright lights in a world full of crooked and perverse people.

(Philippians 2:14-15; Read Psalm 49)

✝✝

What does the Bible verse or Bible chapter mean to you?

_____

_____

How does complaining harm your Christian witness?

_____

_____

List your PRAYER REQUESTS and PRAY.

☐ _____

☐ _____

☐ _____

☐ _____

What is God teaching you or asking you to do?

_____

_____

Date: _____

Conceit / Haughtiness

Pride goes before destruction, and haughtiness before a fall.
You can identify fools just by the way they walk down the street.

(Proverbs 16:18, Ecclesiastes 10:3; Read Psalm 50)

††

What does the Bible verse or Bible chapter mean to you?

_____

_____

When is pride healthy, and when is pride full of conceit?

_____

_____

List your PRAYER REQUESTS and PRAY.

☐ _____

☐ _____

☐ _____

☐ _____

What is God teaching you or asking you to do?

_____

_____

Date: _____

Covetousness

For the commandments say, "You must not commit adultery.
You must not murder. You must not steal. You must not covet."
These – and other such commandments – are summed up in
this one commandment: "Love your neighbor as yourself."

(Romans 13:9; Read Psalm 51)

††

What does the Bible verse or Bible chapter mean to you?

_____

_____

Have you ever wanted something someone else had? What was it?

_____

_____

List your PRAYER REQUESTS and PRAY.

☐ _____

☐ _____

☐ _____

☐ _____

What is God teaching you or asking you to do?

_____

_____

Date: _____

Gossip

A gossip goes around telling secrets,
but those who are trustworthy can keep a confidence.

(Proverbs 11:13; Read Psalm 52)

††

What does the Bible verse or Bible chapter mean to you?

_____
_____

How do you react when you encounter gossip?

_____
_____

List your PRAYER REQUESTS and PRAY.

☐ _____
☐ _____
☐ _____
☐ _____

What is God teaching you or asking you to do?

_____
_____

Date: _____

Ingratitude

Be thankful in all circumstances, for this is God's will
for you who belong to Christ Jesus.

(1 Thessalonians 5:18; Read Psalm 53)

✝✝

What does the Bible verse or Bible chapter mean to you?

_____

_____

Describe a time you thanked God for what He has given you.

_____

_____

List your PRAYER REQUESTS and PRAY.

☐ _____

☐ _____

☐ _____

☐ _____

What is God teaching you or asking you to do?

_____

_____

Date: _____

Judging Others

Jesus said, "Look beneath the surface so you can judge correctly."

(John 7:24; Read Psalm 54)

††

What does the Bible verse or Bible chapter mean to you?

_____

_____

Why should you hesitate or think twice before judging others?

_____

_____

List your PRAYER REQUESTS and PRAY.

☐ _____

☐ _____

☐ _____

☐ _____

What is God teaching you or asking you to do?

_____

_____

Date: _____

Pride

Pride ends in humiliation, while humility brings honor.

(Proverbs 29:23; Read Psalm 55)

††

What does the Bible verse or Bible chapter mean to you?

_____

_____

Describe a time when God humbled you. What did you learn?

_____

_____

List your PRAYER REQUESTS and PRAY.

☐ _____

☐ _____

☐ _____

☐ _____

What is God teaching you or asking you to do?

_____

_____

Date: _____

Self-Control

A person without self-control
is like a city with broken-down walls.

(Proverbs 25:28; Read Psalm 56)

††

What does the Bible verse or Bible chapter mean to you?

_____

_____

What situations in your life cause you to need more self-control?

_____

_____

List your PRAYER REQUESTS and PRAY.

☐ _____

☐ _____

☐ _____

☐ _____

What is God teaching you or asking you to do?

_____

_____

Date: _____

Your Tongue

People can tame all kinds of animals, birds, reptiles, and fish, but no one can tame the tongue. It is restless and evil, full of deadly poison. Sometimes it praises our Lord and Father, and sometimes it curses those who have been made in the image of God.

(James 3:7-9; Read Psalm 57)

††

What does the Bible verse or Bible chapter mean to you?

_____

_____

How do you feel when someone says something nice about you?

_____

_____

List your PRAYER REQUESTS and PRAY.

☐ _____

☐ _____

☐ _____

☐ _____

What is God teaching you or asking you to do?

_____

_____

Date: _____

Your Words

Kind words are like honey—
sweet to the soul and healthy for the body.

(Proverbs 16:24; Read Psalm 58)

††

What does the Bible verse or Bible chapter mean to you?

_____

_____

How do your words show your character to others?

_____

_____

List your PRAYER REQUESTS and PRAY.

☐ _____

☐ _____

☐ _____

☐ _____

What is God teaching you or asking you to do?

_____

_____

It's Biblical

Bible Study

"My conviction firmly rooted
on the unshifting Rock
That shakes and moves all else,
Calm and confident
Pillar in a gust, possessing my
soul, despite the quakes."

Poetry Credit: *Shine Through*,
Glory C. Odemene ©2014

Date: _____

Backsliding

So we must listen very carefully to the truth we have heard, or
we may drift away from it.

(Hebrews 2:1; Read Psalm 59)

✝✝

What does the Bible verse or Bible chapter mean to you?

_____

_____

Define <u>backsliding</u>. Use a dictionary or digital device.

_____

_____

List your PRAYER REQUESTS and PRAY.

☐ _____

☐ _____

☐ _____

☐ _____

What is God teaching you or asking you to do?

_____

_____

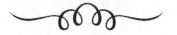

Date: _____

Bible Study

Study this Book of Instruction continually. Meditate on it day
and night so you will be sure to obey everything written in it.
Only then will you prosper and succeed in all you do.

(Joshua 1:8; Read Psalm 60)

††

What does the Bible verse or Bible chapter mean to you?

_____

_____

List 2 ways you can improve your Bible study time.

_____

_____

List your PRAYER REQUESTS and PRAY.

☐ _____

☐ _____

☐ _____

☐ _____

What is God teaching you or asking you to do?

_____

_____

Date: _____

Creationism / Evolution

In the beginning God created the heavens and the earth.

(Genesis 1:1; Read Psalm 61)

✝✝

What does the Bible verse or Bible chapter mean to you?

_____

_____

Why is there a debate between creationism and evolution?

_____

_____

List your PRAYER REQUESTS and PRAY.

☐ _____

☐ _____

☐ _____

☐ _____

What is God teaching you or asking you to do?

_____

_____

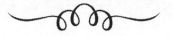

Date: _____

Decision Making

So the Lord must wait for you to come to him so he can show you
his love and compassion…Blessed are those who wait for his help.
Your own ears will hear him. Right behind you a voice will say,
"This is the way you should go," whether to the right or to the left.

(Isaiah 30:18, 21; Read Psalm 62)

✝✝✝

What does the Bible verse or Bible chapter mean to you?

_____

_____

What major decisions are you facing? Have you prayed about them?

_____

_____

List your PRAYER REQUESTS and PRAY.

☐ _____

☐ _____

☐ _____

☐ _____

What is God teaching you or asking you to do?

_____

_____

Date: _____

Discipline

No discipline is enjoyable while it is happening—it's painful!
But afterward there will be a peaceful harvest of right living
for those who are trained in this way.

(Hebrews 12:11; Read Psalm 63)

††

What does the Bible verse or Bible chapter mean to you?

_____

_____

How do you feel when you are disciplined? Give an example.

_____

_____

List your PRAYER REQUESTS and PRAY.

☐ _____

☐ _____

☐ _____

☐ _____

What is God teaching you or asking you to do?

_____

_____

Date: _____

Discrimination / Racism

There is no longer Jew or Gentile, slave or free,
male and female. For you are all one in Christ Jesus.

(Galatians 3:28; Read Psalm 64)

✝✝

What does the Bible verse or Bible chapter mean to you?

_____

_____

Why do you think it is so hard for us to love each other?

_____

_____

List your PRAYER REQUESTS and PRAY.

☐ _____

☐ _____

☐ _____

☐ _____

What is God teaching you or asking you to do?

_____

_____

_____

Date: _____

End Times

However, no one knows the day or hour when these things will
happen, not even the angels in heaven or the Son himself.
Only the Father knows.

(Matthew 24:36; Read Psalm 65)

††

What does the Bible verse or Bible chapter mean to you?

_____

_____

Have you ever studied the end times prophesies in the Bible?

_____

_____

List your PRAYER REQUESTS and PRAY.

☐ _____

☐ _____

☐ _____

☐ _____

What is God teaching you or asking you to do?

_____

_____

Date: _____

Favoritism

But if you favor some people over others, you are committing a sin.
You are guilty of breaking the law.

(James 2:9; Read Psalm 66)

†††

What does the Bible verse or Bible chapter mean to you?

_____

_____

Describe a time you observed favoritism in action. How did you feel?

_____

_____

List your PRAYER REQUESTS and PRAY.

☐ _____

☐ _____

☐ _____

☐ _____

What is God teaching you or asking you to do?

_____

_____

Date: _____

Forgiveness

I – Yes, I alone – will blot out your sins for my own sake
and will never think of them again.

(Isaiah 43:25; Read Psalm 67)

††

What does the Bible verse or Bible chapter mean to you?

_____

_____

How does it feel when someone asks you to forgive them?

_____

_____

List your PRAYER REQUESTS and PRAY.

☐ _____

☐ _____

☐ _____

☐ _____

What is God teaching you or asking you to do?

_____

_____

Date: _____

Fortune-telling / Witchcraft

Do not practice fortune-telling or witchcraft.

(Leviticus 19:26b; Read Psalm 68)

††

What does the Bible verse or Bible chapter mean to you?

_____

_____

How can fortune-telling and witchcraft lead us away from God?

_____

_____

List your PRAYER REQUESTS and PRAY.

☐ _____

☐ _____

☐ _____

☐ _____

What is God teaching you or asking you to do?

_____

_____

Date: _____

Lying

The LORD detests lying lips,
but he delights in those who tell the truth.

(Proverbs 12:22; Read Psalm 69)

✝✝✝

What does the Bible verse or Bible chapter mean to you?

_____

_____

Why should parents be concerned if their children continually lie?

_____

_____

List your PRAYER REQUESTS and PRAY.

☐ _____

☐ _____

☐ _____

☐ _____

What is God teaching you or asking you to do?

_____

_____

Date: _____

Managing Your Life

The Lord says, "I will guide you along the best pathway for your life.
I will advise you and watch over you."

(Psalm 32:8; Read Psalm 70)

††

What does the Bible verse or Bible chapter mean to you?

_____

_____

Are you following God's plan for your life? Why or why not?

_____

_____

List your PRAYER REQUESTS and PRAY.

☐ _____

☐ _____

☐ _____

☐ _____

What is God teaching you or asking you to do?

_____

_____

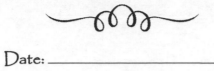

Date: _____

Mediums

Do not defile yourselves by turning to mediums or to those
who consult the spirits of the dead. I am the Lord your God.

(Leviticus 19:31; Read Psalm 71)

††

What does the Bible verse or Bible chapter mean to you?

_____

_____

What are some examples of mediums in our society today?

_____

_____

List your PRAYER REQUESTS and PRAY.

☐ _____

☐ _____

☐ _____

☐ _____

What is God teaching you or asking you to do?

_____

_____

Date: _____

Mockery

God blesses you when people mock you and persecute you and
lie about you and say all sorts of evil things against you
because you are my followers. Be happy about it!
Be very glad! For a great reward awaits you in Heaven.

(Matthew 5:11-12a; Read Psalm 72)

††

What does the Bible verse or Bible chapter mean to you?

_____

_____

Define <u>mockery</u>. Use a dictionary or digital device.

_____

_____

List your PRAYER REQUESTS and PRAY.

☐ _____

☐ _____

☐ _____

☐ _____

What is God teaching you or asking you to do?

_____

_____

Date: _____

Money

Don't love money; be satisfied with what you have.
For God has said,
"I will never fail you.
I will never abandon you."

(Hebrews 13:5; Read Psalm 73)

✝✝

What does the Bible verse or Bible chapter mean to you?

_____

_____

Why is the "love of money" destructive?

_____

_____

List your PRAYER REQUESTS and PRAY.

☐ _____

☐ _____

☐ _____

☐ _____

What is God teaching you or asking you to do?

_____

_____

Movies and Television

I will be careful to live a blameless life
—when will you come to help me?
I will lead a life of integrity in my own home.
I will refuse to look at anything vile and vulgar.

(Psalm 101:2-3a; Read Psalm 74)

††

What does the Bible verse or Bible chapter mean to you?

_____

_____

Should movies contain immoral content? Why or why not?

_____

_____

List your PRAYER REQUESTS and PRAY.

☐ _____

☐ _____

☐ _____

☐ _____

What is God teaching you or asking you to do?

_____

_____

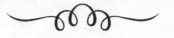

Date: _____

Rebellion

But if you rebel against the Lord's commands and refuse
to listen to him, then his hand will be as
heavy upon you as it was upon your ancestors.

(1 Samuel 12:15; Read Psalm 75)

††

What does the Bible verse or Bible chapter mean to you?

_____

_____

Define <u>rebellion</u>. Use a dictionary or digital device.

_____

_____

List your PRAYER REQUESTS and PRAY.

- ☐ _____
- ☐ _____
- ☐ _____
- ☐ _____

What is God teaching you or asking you to do?

_____

_____

Date: _____

Stealing

And Jesus replied: "You must not murder. You must not commit adultery. You must not steal. You must not testify falsely. Honor your father and mother. Love your neighbor as yourself."

(Matthew 19:18b-19; Read Psalm 76)

††

What does the Bible verse or Bible chapter mean to you?

_____

_____

Describe how stealing hurts its victims.

_____

_____

List your PRAYER REQUESTS and PRAY.

☐ _____

☐ _____

☐ _____

☐ _____

What is God teaching you or asking you to do?

_____

_____

Date: _____

Suffering

For he has not ignored or belittled the suffering of the needy.
He has not turned his back on them,
but has listened to their cries for help.

(Psalm 22:24; Read Psalm 77)

††

What does the Bible verse or Bible chapter mean to you?

_____

_____

Describe a time you or someone you love suffered.

_____

_____

List your PRAYER REQUESTS and PRAY.

☐ _____

☐ _____

☐ _____

☐ _____

What is God teaching you or asking you to do?

_____

_____

Date: _____

Trials

Dear brothers and sisters, when troubles come your way,
consider it an opportunity for great joy. For you know that when
your faith is tested, your endurance has a chance to grow.

(James 1:2-3; Read Psalm 78)

††

What does the Bible verse or Bible chapter mean to you?

_____

_____

Describe a trial you have encountered, and how you grew from it.

_____

_____

List your PRAYER REQUESTS and PRAY.

☐ _____

☐ _____

☐ _____

☐ _____

What is God teaching you or asking you to do?

_____

_____

It's Issues

An Alcoholic

"To an observer, it is tough work but to me
I am paying in advance, [a] very dear price
In hope of winning a much dearer prize
I train to win, ignoring the enticements
Of exotic interests, counting them for now
As nothing but distractions, obstructions . . ."

Poetry Credit: *The Race,* Glory
C. Odemene ©2013

Date: _____

Addictions / Strongholds

The temptations in your life are no different from what others experience. And God is faithful. He will not allow the temptation to be more than you can stand. When you are tempted, he will show you a way out so that you can endure.

(1 Corinthians 10:13; Read Psalm 79)

✝✝✝

What does the Bible verse or Bible chapter mean to you?

_____

_____

How do drugs become an addiction?

_____

_____

List your PRAYER REQUESTS and PRAY.

☐ _____

☐ _____

☐ _____

☐ _____

What is God teaching you or asking you to do?

_____

_____

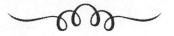

Date: _____

Cutting ~ Tattoos

Do not cut your bodies for the dead, and do not mark
your skin with tattoos. I am the Lord.

(Leviticus 19:28; Read Psalm 80)

✝✝✝

What does the Bible verse or Bible chapter mean to you?

_____

_____

Why is cutting and tattooing a controversial topic?

_____

_____

List your PRAYER REQUESTS and PRAY.

- ☐ _____
- ☐ _____
- ☐ _____
- ☐ _____

What is God teaching you or asking you to do?

_____

_____

Date: _____

Death of a Loved One

God blesses those who mourn, for they will be comforted.

(Matthew 5:4; Read Psalm 81)

††

What does the Bible verse or Bible chapter mean to you?

_____

_____

How do you comfort someone who has lost a loved one?

_____

_____

List your PRAYER REQUESTS and PRAY.

☐ _____

☐ _____

☐ _____

☐ _____

What is God teaching you or asking you to do?

_____

_____

Date: _____

Drug Addiction / Prescription Pain Pills

Peter said, "For you are a slave to whatever controls you."

(2 Peter 2:19b; Read Psalm 82)

✝✝✝

What does the Bible verse or Bible chapter mean to you?

_____

_____

How does drug addiction start? How does it control people?

_____

_____

List your PRAYER REQUESTS and PRAY.

☐ _____

☐ _____

☐ _____

☐ _____

What is God teaching you or asking you to do?

_____

_____

Date: _____

Eating Disorders

There [Jesus] told them, "Pray that you will not give in to temptation."

(Luke 22:40; Read Psalm 83)

††

What does the Bible verse or Bible chapter mean to you?

_____

_____

In your opinion, why are some people obsessed with their weight?

_____

_____

List your PRAYER REQUESTS and PRAY.

☐ _____

☐ _____

☐ _____

☐ _____

What is God teaching you or asking you to do?

_____

_____

Date: _____

Homelessness

Don't be afraid, for I am with you.
Don't be discouraged, for I am your God.
I will strengthen you and help you.
I will hold you up with my victorious right hand.

(Isaiah 41:10; Read Psalm 84)

††

What does the Bible verse or Bible chapter mean to you?

_____

_____

Recall an encounter you have had with a homeless person.

_____

_____

List your PRAYER REQUESTS and PRAY.

- ☐ _____
- ☐ _____
- ☐ _____
- ☐ _____

What is God teaching you or asking you to do?

_____

_____

Date: _____

Internet

So be careful how you live. Don't live like fools,
but like those who are wise.
Make the most of every opportunity in these evil days.

(Ephesians 5:15-16; Read Psalm 85)

††

What does the Bible verse or Bible chapter mean to you?

_____

_____

What dangers might we encounter when using the Internet?

_____

_____

List your PRAYER REQUESTS and PRAY.

☐ _____

☐ _____

☐ _____

☐ _____

What is God teaching you or asking you to do?

_____

_____

Date: _____

Moving

Moses, Speaking to the Israelites in the desert, said: "So be strong
and courageous! Do not be afraid and do not panic before them.
For the Lord your God will personally go ahead of you.
He will neither fail you nor abandon you."

(Deuteronomy 31:6; Read Psalm 86)

††

What does the Bible verse or Bible chapter mean to you?

_____

_____

Have you ever moved? How did it affect you?

_____

_____

List your PRAYER REQUESTS and PRAY.

☐ _____

☐ _____

☐ _____

☐ _____

What is God teaching you or asking you to do?

_____

_____

Date: _____

Poverty

Feed the hungry, and help those in trouble.
Then your light will shine out from the darkness,
and the darkness around you will be as bright as noon.

(Isaiah 58:10; Read Psalm 87)

††

What does the Bible verse or Bible chapter mean to you?

_____

_____

What are the effects of poverty, if any, in your community?

_____

_____

List your PRAYER REQUESTS and PRAY.

☐ _____

☐ _____

☐ _____

☐ _____

What is God teaching you or asking you to do?

_____

_____

Date: _____

Runaway

The Lord is a shelter for the
oppressed, a refuge in times of trouble.
Those who know your name trust in you, for you,
O Lord, do not abandon those who search for you.

(Psalm 9:9-10; Read Psalm 88)

✝✝✝

What does the Bible verse or Bible chapter mean to you?

_____

_____

What are children and teenagers looking for when they run away?

_____

_____

List your PRAYER REQUESTS and PRAY.

☐ _____

☐ _____

☐ _____

☐ _____

What is God teaching you or asking you to do?

_____

_____

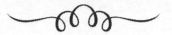

Date: _____

Self-Destruction

Don't you realize that all of you together are the temple of God and
that the Spirit of God lives in you? God will
destroy anyone who destroys this temple.
For God's temple is holy, and you are that temple.

(1 Corinthians 3:16-17; Read Psalm 89)

✝✝✝

What does the Bible verse or Bible chapter mean to you?

_____

_____

Why do you think God doesn't want us to hurt ourselves?

_____

_____

List your PRAYER REQUESTS and PRAY.

☐ _____

☐ _____

☐ _____

☐ _____

What is God teaching you or asking you to do?

_____

_____

Date: _____

Sex Addiction

"I have seen what they do, but I will heal them anyway! I
will lead them. I will comfort those who mourn, bringing
words of praise to their lips. May they have abundant peace,
both near and far, says the Lord, who heals them."

(Isaiah 57:18-19; Read Psalm 90)

††

What does the Bible verse or Bible chapter mean to you?

_____

_____

What do you feel is the root cause of sex addiction?

_____

_____

List your PRAYER REQUESTS and PRAY.

☐ _____

☐ _____

☐ _____

☐ _____

What is God teaching you or asking you to do?

_____

_____

Date: _____

Self-Image / Appearance

Don't be concerned about the outward beauty of fancy hairstyles,
expensive jewelry, or beautiful clothes. You should clothe yourselves
instead with the beauty that comes from within, the unfading
beauty of a gentle and quiet spirit, which is so precious to God.

(1 Peter 3:3-4; Read Psalm 91)

††

What does the Bible verse or Bible chapter mean to you?

_____

_____

Why do some people place so much value on outward appearances?

_____

_____

List your PRAYER REQUESTS and PRAY.

☐ _____

☐ _____

☐ _____

☐ _____

What is God teaching you or asking you to do?

_____

_____

Date: _____

Smoking/Tobacco

Rather, clothe yourselves with the Lord Jesus Christ, and do not think about how to gratify the desires of the flesh.

(Romans 13:14 NIV; Read Psalm 92)

†††

What does the Bible verse or Bible chapter mean to you?

_____

_____

If people know smoking is unhealthy, why do they continue to smoke?

_____

_____

List your PRAYER REQUESTS and PRAY.

☐ _____

☐ _____

☐ _____

☐ _____

What is God teaching you or asking you to do?

_____

_____

_____

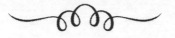

Date: _____

Social Media

Dear children, keep away from anything that might
take God's place in your hearts.

(1 John 5:21; Read Psalm 93)

✝✝✝

What does the Bible verse or Bible chapter mean to you?

_____

_____

Do you have any photos or texts you wish you could "un-post"?

_____

_____

List your PRAYER REQUESTS and PRAY.

☐ _____

☐ _____

☐ _____

☐ _____

What is God teaching you or asking you to do?

_____

_____

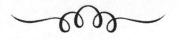

Date: _____

Suicide

Said Moses to the Israelites in the desert, "Today I have given you the choice between life and death, between blessings and curses. Now I call on heaven and earth to witness the choice you make. Oh, that you would choose life, so that you and your descendants might live!"

(Deuteronomy 30:19; Read Psalm 94)

✝✝✝

What does the Bible verse or Bible chapter mean to you?

_____

_____

Why is suicide not the answer to life's problems?

_____

_____

List your PRAYER REQUESTS and PRAY.

☐ _____

☐ _____

☐ _____

☐ _____

What is God teaching you or asking you to do?

_____

_____

Date: _____

Terrorists

[God] abandoned them to their foolish thinking and let them
do things that should never be done. Their lives became full
of every kind of wickedness, sin, greed, hate, envy, murder,
quarreling, deception, malicious behavior, and gossip. They are
backstabbers, haters of God, insolent, proud, and boastful. They
invent new ways of sinning, and they disobey their parents.

(Romans 1:28b-31: Read Psalm 95)

††

What does the Bible verse or Bible chapter mean to you?

_____

_____

How should a believer respond to terrorism?

_____

_____

List your PRAYER REQUESTS and PRAY.

☐ _____

☐ _____

☐ _____

☐ _____

What is God teaching you or asking you to do?

_____

_____

Date: _____

Time Management

For everything there is a season, a time for every activity under heaven.

(Ecclesiastes 3:1; Read Psalm 96)

††

What does the Bible verse or Bible chapter mean to you?

_____

_____

What are some interruptions or distractions that you face daily?

_____

_____

List your PRAYER REQUESTS and PRAY.

☐ _____

☐ _____

☐ _____

☐ _____

What is God teaching you or asking you to do?

_____

_____

Date: _____

Violence

The Lord examines both the righteous and the wicked.
He hates those who love violence.

(Psalm 11:5; Read Psalm 97)

†††

What does the Bible verse or Bible chapter mean to you?

_____

_____

Have we as a society become desensitized to violence? Explain.

_____

_____

List your PRAYER REQUESTS and PRAY.

☐ _____

☐ _____

☐ _____

☐ _____

What is God teaching you or asking you to do?

_____

_____

Date: _____

War

O Lord, oppose those who oppose me.
Fight those who fight against me.
Put on your armor, and take up your shield.
Prepare for battle, and come to my aid.

(Psalm 35:1-2; Read Psalm 98)

✝✝✝

What does the Bible verse or Bible chapter mean to you?

_____

_____

Why do we as humans go to war with one another?

_____

_____

List your PRAYER REQUESTS and PRAY.

☐ _____

☐ _____

☐ _____

☐ _____

What is God teaching you or asking you to do?

_____

_____

It's Illegal

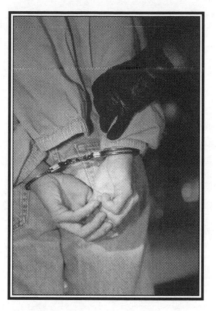

Teenage Boy getting Handcuffed

Attempts to be like others wrought miseries
Trying to fit [in], I proved a
misfit, repelling those
I meant to attract. Worn out at last, I gave up.
Lying at His feet, I sought His face, His will:
"Do with me as it seems best in Your sight.
On my own, I am no good
and I can't fit [in] . . ."

Poetry Credit:, *Cracks*, Glory
C. Odemene ©2013

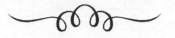

Date: _____

Alcohol Use

Wine produces mockers; alcohol leads to brawls.
Those led astray by drink cannot be wise.

(Proverbs 20:1; Read Psalm 99)

††

What does the Bible verse or Bible chapter mean to you?

_____

_____

What consequences are associated with excessive drinking?

_____

_____

List your PRAYER REQUESTS and PRAY.

☐ _____

☐ _____

☐ _____

☐ _____

What is God teaching you or asking you to do?

_____

_____

Bullying, Online and Offline

Don't be selfish; don't try to impress others. Be humble, thinking of others as better than yourselves. Don't look out only for your own interests, but take an interest in others, too.

(Philippians 2:3-4; Read Psalm 100)

††

What does the Bible verse or Bible chapter mean to you?

_____

_____

Describe the harmful effects of bullying on the victim.

_____

_____

List your PRAYER REQUESTS and PRAY.

- ☐ _____
- ☐ _____
- ☐ _____
- ☐ _____

What is God teaching you or asking you to do?

_____

_____

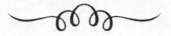

Date: _____

Drugs / Performance Enhancing Drugs

You say, "I am allowed to do anything" – but
not everything is good for you.
You say, "I am allowed to do anything"
–but not everything is beneficial.

(1 Corinthians 10:23; Read Psalm 101)

††

What does the Bible verse or Bible chapter mean to you?

_____

_____

What are some of the harmful effects of legal and illegal drugs?

_____

_____

List your PRAYER REQUESTS and PRAY.

- ☐ _____
- ☐ _____
- ☐ _____
- ☐ _____

What is God teaching you or asking you to do?

_____

_____

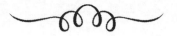

Date: _____

Murder

You must not murder.

(Exodus 20:13; Read Psalm 102)

††
What does the Bible verse or Bible chapter mean to you?

_____

_____

What should be the punishment for someone who commits murder?

_____

_____

List your PRAYER REQUESTS and PRAY.

☐ _____

☐ _____

☐ _____

☐ _____

What is God teaching you or asking you to do?

_____

_____

Date: _____

Physical Abuse

The Lord replies, "I have seen violence done to
the helpless, and I have heard the groans of the poor.
Now I will rise up to rescue them,
as they have longed for me to do."

(Psalm 12:5; Read Psalm 103)

✝✝

What does the Bible verse or Bible chapter mean to you?

_____

_____

Have you known anyone physically assaulted? Did they receive help?

_____

_____

List your PRAYER REQUESTS and PRAY.

- ☐ _____
- ☐ _____
- ☐ _____
- ☐ _____

What is God teaching you or asking you to do?

_____

_____

Date: _____

Pornography

Then I said to them, 'Each of you, get rid of the vile images
you are so obsessed with. Do not defile yourselves with
the idols of Egypt, for I am the LORD your God.'

(Ezekiel 20:7; Read Psalm 104)

††

What does the Bible verse or Bible chapter mean to you?

_____

_____

What do you think is the root cause of pornography?

_____

_____

List your PRAYER REQUESTS and PRAY.

☐ _____

☐ _____

☐ _____

☐ _____

What is God teaching you or asking you to do?

_____

_____

Date: _____

Sexting

Let there be no sexual immorality, impurity, or greed among you.
Such sins have no place among God's people. Obscene
stories, foolish talk, and coarse jokes—these are not for
you. Instead, let there be thankfulness to God.

(Ephesians 5:3-4; Read Psalm 105)

††

What does the Bible verse or Bible chapter mean to you?

_____

_____

Why does God consider sexting as "sexually immoral"?

_____

_____

List your PRAYER REQUESTS and PRAY.

☐ _____

☐ _____

☐ _____

☐ _____

What is God teaching you or asking you to do?

_____

_____

It's Spiritual

A Man Reading the Bible

"O the joyful
Relief that dreams come true, that my
Hope yet lives
That forever He lives, He rules: it can
Only be imagined!"

Poetry Credit: *I Can Only Imagine*,
Glory C. Odemene ©2014

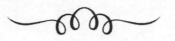

Angels

For he will order his angels
to protect you wherever you go.

Psalm 91:11; Read Psalm 106)

✝✝✝

What does the Bible verse or Bible chapter mean to you?

_____

_____

The Bible says there are angels. Why should you believe God's Word?

_____

_____

List your PRAYER REQUESTS and PRAY.

☐ _____

☐ _____

☐ _____

☐ _____

What is God teaching you or asking you to do?

_____

_____

Date: _____

Ask God

Keep on asking, and you will receive what you ask for. Keep on
seeking, and you will find. Keep on knocking, and the door will
be opened to you. For everyone who asks, receives. Everyone who
seeks, finds. And to everyone who knocks, the door will be opened.

(Matthew 7:7-8; Read Psalm 107)

††

What does the Bible verse or Bible chapter mean to you?

_____

_____

If you have one main request for God today, what would it be?

_____

_____

List your PRAYER REQUESTS and PRAY.

☐ _____

☐ _____

☐ _____

☐ _____

What is God teaching you or asking you to do?

_____

_____

Date: _____

Believe

If you confess with your mouth that Jesus is Lord and believe in
your heart that God raised him from the dead, you will be saved.
For it is by believing in your heart that you are made right with
God, and it is by confessing with your mouth that you are saved.

(Romans 10:9-10; Read Psalm 108)

††

What does the Bible verse or Bible chapter mean to you?

_____

_____

What is your relationship with Jesus?

_____

_____

List your PRAYER REQUESTS and PRAY.

- ☐ _____
- ☐ _____
- ☐ _____
- ☐ _____

What is God teaching you or asking you to do?

_____

_____

Date: _____

Church Attendance

And let us not neglect our meeting together, as some people do,
but encourage one another, especially now that
the day of his return is drawing near.

(Hebrews 10:25; Read Psalm 109)

††

What does the Bible verse or Bible chapter mean to you?

_____

_____

Name 2 reasons attending church is beneficial.

_____

_____

List your PRAYER REQUESTS and PRAY.

☐ _____

☐ _____

☐ _____

☐ _____

What is God teaching you or asking you to do?

_____

_____

Date: _____

Evangelism

Therefore, go and make disciples of all the nations, baptizing them
in the name of the Father and the Son and the Holy Spirit.

(Matthew 28:19; Read Psalm 110)

††

What does the Bible verse or Bible chapter mean to you?

_____

_____

Do you feel prepared to share God with others? Explain.

_____

_____

List your PRAYER REQUESTS and PRAY.

- ☐ _____
- ☐ _____
- ☐ _____
- ☐ _____

What is God teaching you or asking you to do?

_____

_____

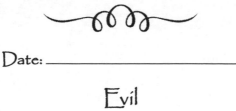

Date: _____

Evil

Don't let evil conquer you, but conquer evil by doing good.

(Romans 12:21; Read Psalm 111)

††

What does the Bible verse or Bible chapter mean to you?

_____

_____

How can you "conquer evil" by doing good today?

_____

_____

List your PRAYER REQUESTS and PRAY.

☐ _____

☐ _____

☐ _____

☐ _____

What is God teaching you or asking you to do?

_____

_____

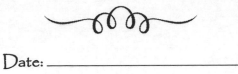

Date: _____

Faith

Faith is the confidence that what we hope for will actually happen;
it gives us assurance about things we cannot see.

(Hebrews 11:1; Read Psalm 112)

††

What does the Bible verse or Bible chapter mean to you?

_____

_____

Describe a time you shared your faith with another person.

_____

_____

List your PRAYER REQUESTS and PRAY.

☐ _____

☐ _____

☐ _____

☐ _____

What is God teaching you or asking you to do?

_____

_____

Date: _____

Forgive

Jesus said, "But when you are praying, first forgive anyone
you are holding a grudge against, so that your
Father in heaven will forgive your sins, too."

(Mark 11:25; Read Psalm 113)

††
What does the Bible verse or Bible chapter mean to you?

_____

_____

Is it easy or hard to forgive those who hurt you? Why or why not?

_____

_____

List your PRAYER REQUESTS and PRAY.

☐ _____

☐ _____

☐ _____

☐ _____

What is God teaching you or asking you to do?

_____

_____

Date: _____

Fruit of the Spirit

But the Holy Spirit produces this kind of fruit in our lives: love, joy, peace, patience, kindness, goodness, faithfulness, gentleness, and self-control. There is no law against these things!

(Galatians 5:22-23; Read Psalm 114)

††

What does the Bible verse or Bible chapter mean to you?

_____

_____

List five "Fruits of the Spirit" mentioned in the verse above.

_____

_____

List your PRAYER REQUESTS and PRAY.

☐ _____

☐ _____

☐ _____

☐ _____

What is God teaching you or asking you to do?

_____

_____

Date: _____

God Understands

This High Priest of ours understands our weaknesses, for he faced
all of the same testings we do, yet he did not sin. So let us come
boldly to the throne of our gracious God. There we will receive his
mercy, and we will find grace to help us when we need it most.

(Hebrews 4:15-16; Read Psalm 115)

††
What does the Bible verse or Bible chapter mean to you?

_____

_____

Describe a time when you felt no one understood you.

_____

_____

List your PRAYER REQUESTS and PRAY.

- ☐ _____
- ☐ _____
- ☐ _____
- ☐ _____

What is God teaching you or asking you to do?

_____

_____

Date: _____

God's Will

So the LORD must wait for you to come to him so
he can show you his love and compassion…
Your own ears will hear him. Right behind you a voice will say,
"This is the way you should go," whether to the right or to the left.

(Isaiah 30:18a, 21; Read Psalm 116)

††

What does the Bible verse or Bible chapter mean to you?

_____

_____

Describe a time you waited upon God for an answer.

_____

_____

List your PRAYER REQUESTS and PRAY.

☐ _____

☐ _____

☐ _____

☐ _____

What is God teaching you or asking you to do?

_____

_____

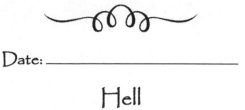

Date: _____

Hell

You can enter God's Kingdom only through the narrow gate.
The highway to hell is broad, and
its gate is wide for the many who choose that way.

(Matthew 7:13; Read Psalm 117)

††

What does the Bible verse or Bible chapter mean to you?

_____

_____

What is your opinion about an afterlife in either heaven or hell?

_____

_____

List your PRAYER REQUESTS and PRAY.

☐ _____

☐ _____

☐ _____

☐ _____

What is God teaching you or asking you to do?

_____

_____

Date: _____

Holy Spirit

Let me ask you this one question: Did you receive the Holy Spirit by obeying the law of Moses? Of course not! You received the Spirit because you believed the message you heard about Christ.

(Galatians 3:2; Read Psalm 118)

††

What does the Bible verse or Bible chapter mean to you?

_____

_____

What do you know about the Holy Spirit?

_____

_____

List your PRAYER REQUESTS and PRAY.

☐ _____

☐ _____

☐ _____

☐ _____

What is God teaching you or asking you to do?

_____

_____

Date: _____

Miracles

"He rescues and saves his people; he performs miraculous
signs and wonders in the heavens and on earth.
He has rescued Daniel from the power of the lions."
(King Darius, in a message to the people of the
World about the God of Daniel.)

(Daniel 6:27; Read Psalm 119)

††

What does the Bible verse or Bible chapter mean to you?

_____

_____

Do you believe miracles are possible? Explain why or why not.

_____

_____

List your PRAYER REQUESTS and PRAY.

- ☐ _____
- ☐ _____
- ☐ _____
- ☐ _____

What is God teaching you or asking you to do?

_____

_____

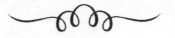

Date: _____

Obedience

So Moses told the people, "You must be careful to obey all the commands of the LORD your God, following his instructions in every detail. Stay on the path that the Lord your God has commanded you to follow. Then you will live long and prosperous lives in the land you are about to enter and occupy."

(Deuteronomy 5:32-33; Read Psalm 120)

††

What does the Bible verse or Bible chapter mean to you?

_____

_____

How can you make obeying God a priority in your life?

_____

_____

List your PRAYER REQUESTS and PRAY.

☐ _____

☐ _____

☐ _____

☐ _____

What is God teaching you or asking you to do?

_____

_____

Date: _____

Patience

We also pray that you will be strengthened with all his glorious
power so you will have all the endurance and patience you need.
May you be filled with joy, always thanking the Father.

(Colossians 1:11-12a; Read Psalm 121)

††

What does the Bible verse or Bible chapter mean to you?

_____

_____

Are you waiting patiently for God to act in any situations? Explain.

_____

_____

List your PRAYER REQUESTS and PRAY.

☐ _____

☐ _____

☐ _____

☐ _____

What is God teaching you or asking you to do?

_____

_____

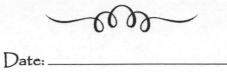

Date: _____

Prayer

Don't worry about anything; instead, pray about everything.
Tell God what you need, and thank him for all he has done.

(Philippians 4:6; Read Psalm 122)

††

What does the Bible verse or Bible chapter mean to you?

_____

_____

Do you pray daily? Why or why not?

_____

_____

List your PRAYER REQUESTS and PRAY.

☐ _____

☐ _____

☐ _____

☐ _____

What is God teaching you or asking you to do?

_____

_____

Date: _____

Resurrection

Jesus told her, "I am the resurrection and the life.
Anyone who believes in me will live, even after dying.
Everyone who lives in me and believes in me will never ever die . . ."

(John 11:25-26a; Read Psalm 123)

††

What does the Bible verse or Bible chapter mean to you?

_____

_____

Why is Jesus' resurrection important in your walk with God?

_____

_____

List your PRAYER REQUESTS and PRAY.

☐ _____

☐ _____

☐ _____

☐ _____

What is God teaching you or asking you to do?

_____

_____

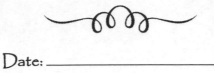

Date: _____

Satan

Stay alert! Watch out for your great enemy, the devil. He prowls
around like a roaring lion, looking for someone to devour.
Stand firm against him, and be strong in your faith.

(1 Peter 5:8-9a; Read Psalm 124)

†††

What does the Bible verse or Bible chapter mean to you?

_____

_____

Who has control in your life—God or Satan? Explain.

_____

_____

List your PRAYER REQUESTS and PRAY.

☐ _____

☐ _____

☐ _____

☐ _____

What is God teaching you or asking you to do?

_____

_____

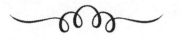

Date: _____

Scriptures

All Scripture is inspired by God and is useful to teach us what is true and to make us realize what is wrong in our lives. It corrects us when we are wrong and teaches us to do what is right. God uses it to prepare and equip his people to do every good work.

(2 Timothy 3:16-17; Read Psalm 125)

✝✝

What does the Bible verse or Bible chapter mean to you?

_____

_____

Name one way the Bible has guided your life.

_____

_____

List your PRAYER REQUESTS and PRAY.

☐ _____

☐ _____

☐ _____

☐ _____

What is God teaching you or asking you to do?

_____

_____

Date: _____

Spiritual Blasphemy

Jesus said, "Anyone who speaks against the Son of Man can be forgiven, but anyone who speaks against the Holy Spirit will never be forgiven, either in this world or in the world to come."

(Matthew 12:32; Read Psalm 126)

✝✝✝

What does the Bible verse or Bible chapter mean to you?

_____

_____

Define <u>blasphemy</u>. Use a dictionary or digital device.

_____

_____

List your PRAYER REQUESTS and PRAY.

☐ _____

☐ _____

☐ _____

☐ _____

What is God teaching you or asking you to do?

_____

_____

Date: _____

Spiritual Gifts

There are different kinds of spiritual gifts, but the same Spirit is
the source of them all. There are different kinds
of service, but we serve the same Lord…A spiritual gift is given to
each of us so we can help each other.

(1 Corinthians 12:4-5, 7; Read Psalm 127)

††

What does the Bible verse or Bible chapter mean to you?

_____

_____

Read 1 Corinthians 12:6-10. Write down four spiritual gifts.

_____

_____

List your PRAYER REQUESTS and PRAY.

☐ _____

☐ _____

☐ _____

☐ _____

What is God teaching you or asking you to do?

_____

_____

Spiritual Maturity

Like newborn babies, you must crave pure spiritual milk
so that you will grow into a full experience of salvation.
Cry out for this nourishment, now that you have had
a taste of the Lord's kindness.

(1 Peter 2:2-3; Read Psalm 128)

††

What does the Bible verse or Bible chapter mean to you?

_____

_____

What are some signs you are beginning to grow spiritually?

_____

_____

List your PRAYER REQUESTS and PRAY.

☐ _____

☐ _____

☐ _____

☐ _____

What is God teaching you or asking you to do?

_____

_____

Date: _____

Spiritual Warfare

A final word: Be strong in the Lord and in his mighty power.
Put on all of God's armor so that you will be able to stand
firm against all strategies of the devil. For we are not fighting
against flesh-and-blood enemies, but against evil rulers and
authorities of the unseen world, against mighty powers in this
dark world, and against evil spirits in the heavenly places.

(Ephesians 6:10-12; Read Psalm 129)

††

What does the Bible verse or Bible chapter mean to you?

_____

_____

Describe a time when you had to choose between good and evil.

_____

_____

List your PRAYER REQUESTS and PRAY.

☐ _____

☐ _____

☐ _____

☐ _____

What is God teaching you or asking you to do?

_____

_____

Date: _____

Spiritual Wisdom

If you need wisdom, ask our generous God,
and he will give it to you. He will not rebuke you for asking.
But when you ask him, be sure that your faith is in God alone.

(James 1:5-6a; Read Psalm 130)

††

What does the Bible verse or Bible chapter mean to you?

_____

_____

Has God ever helped you in solving a problem? Explain.

_____

_____

List your PRAYER REQUESTS and PRAY.

☐ _____

☐ _____

☐ _____

☐ _____

What is God teaching you or asking you to do?

_____

_____

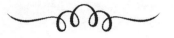

Date: _____

Standing Firm

He called you to salvation when we told you the Good News; now you can share in the glory of our Lord Jesus Christ. With all these things in mind, dear brothers and sisters, stand firm and keep a strong grip on the teaching we passed on to you both in person and by letter.

(2 Thessalonians 2:14-15; (Read Psalm 131)

††

What does the Bible verse or Bible chapter mean to you?

_____

_____

Why should we keep a "strong grip" on God's Word and teachings?

_____

_____

List your PRAYER REQUESTS and PRAY.

- ☐ _____
- ☐ _____
- ☐ _____
- ☐ _____

What is God teaching you or asking you to do?

_____

_____

Date: _____

Standing Up for Others

Speak up for those who cannot speak for themselves;
ensure justice for those being crushed.
Yes, speak up for the poor and helpless,
and see that they get justice.

(Proverbs 31:8-9; Read Psalm 132)

††

What does the Bible verse or Bible chapter mean to you?

_____

_____

Do you have the courage to stand up for someone who is mistreated?

_____

_____

List your PRAYER REQUESTS and PRAY.

☐ _____

☐ _____

☐ _____

☐ _____

What is God teaching you or asking you to do?

_____

_____

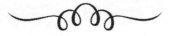

Date: _____

Temptation

The temptations in your life are no different from what others experience. And God is faithful. He will not allow the temptation to be more than you can stand. When you are tempted, he will show you a way out so that you can endure.

(1 Corinthians 10:13; Read Psalm 133)

††

What does the Bible verse or Bible chapter mean to you?

_____

_____

Describe a time you were tempted to do something wrong. Explain.

_____

_____

List your PRAYER REQUESTS and PRAY.

- ☐ _____
- ☐ _____
- ☐ _____
- ☐ _____

What is God teaching you or asking you to do?

_____

_____

Date: _____

Tithing

Bring all the tithes into the storehouse so there will be enough food
in my Temple. If you do, says the LORD of Heaven's Armies, "I will
open the windows of heaven for you. I will pour out a blessing so great
you won't have enough room to take it in! Try it! Put me to the test!"

(Malachi 3:10; Read Psalm 134)

✝✝

What does the Bible verse or Bible chapter mean to you?

_____

_____

Reword the Scripture above in your own words.

_____

_____

List your PRAYER REQUESTS and PRAY.

☐ _____

☐ _____

☐ _____

☐ _____

What is God teaching you or asking you to do?

_____

_____

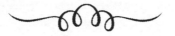

Date: _____

Understanding and Insight

Cry out for insight, and ask for understanding.
Search for them as you would for silver; seek them like
hidden treasures. Then you will understand what it means
to fear the LORD, and you will gain knowledge of God.

(Proverbs 2:3-5; Read Psalm 135)

†††

What does the Bible verse or Bible chapter mean to you?

_____

_____

Describe a situation when you asked God for insight & understanding.

_____

_____

List your PRAYER REQUESTS and PRAY.

- ☐ _____
- ☐ _____
- ☐ _____
- ☐ _____

What is God teaching you or asking you to do?

_____

_____

It's Family

A Three Generation Family standing in a Garden

"Quit the endless hunt for more
Sit back and count my blessings
Look back in time with gratitude
Look up with appreciation
And look around, thankful
For who I am, for where I am."

Poetry Credit: *Thankful*, Glory
C. Odemene ©2013

Date: _____

Adoption

But when the right time came, God sent his Son, born of a woman,
subject to the law. God sent him to buy freedom for us who were
slaves to the law, so that he could adopt us as his very own children.

(Galatians 4:4-5; Read Psalm 136)

✝✝

What does the Bible verse or Bible chapter mean to you?

_____

_____

What does it mean to be adopted?

_____

_____

List your PRAYER REQUESTS and PRAY.

☐ _____

☐ _____

☐ _____

☐ _____

What is God teaching you or asking you to do?

_____

_____

Date: _____

Divorce

Jesus replied, "Moses permitted divorce only as a concession to your hard hearts, but it was not what God had originally intended. And I tell you this, whoever divorces his wife and marries someone else commits adultery—unless his wife has been unfaithful."

(Matthew 19:8-9; Read Psalm 137)

††

What does the Bible verse or Bible chapter mean to you?

_____

_____

How does divorce affect families today?

_____

_____

List your PRAYER REQUESTS and PRAY.

- ☐ _____
- ☐ _____
- ☐ _____
- ☐ _____

What is God teaching you or asking you to do?

_____

_____

Date: _____

Family Illness

God is our merciful Father and the source of all comfort.
He comforts us in all our troubles so that we can comfort others.
When they are troubled, we will be able to give them
the same comfort God has given us.

(2 Corinthians 1:3b-4; Read Psalm 138)

†††

What does the Bible verse or Bible chapter mean to you?

_____

_____

Why do bad things, like serious illnesses, happen to good people?

_____

_____

List your PRAYER REQUESTS and PRAY.

☐ _____

☐ _____

☐ _____

☐ _____

What is God teaching you or asking you to do?

_____

_____

Date: _____

Honor Your Parents

Children, obey your parents because you belong to the Lord, for this is the right thing to do. "Honor your father and mother." This is the first commandment with a promise: If you honor your father and mother, "things will go well for you, and you will have a long life on the earth."

(Ephesians 6:1-3; Read Psalm 139)

†††

What does the Bible verse or Bible chapter mean to you?

_____

_____

How do you treat your parents?

_____

_____

List your PRAYER REQUESTS and PRAY.

☐ _____

☐ _____

☐ _____

☐ _____

What is God teaching you or asking you to do?

_____

_____

Date: _____

Love for Others

Love is patient and kind. Love is not jealous or boastful or
proud or rude. It does not demand its own way. It is not irritable,
and it keeps no record of being wronged. It does not rejoice
about injustice but rejoices whenever the truth wins out.

(1 Corinthians 13:4-6; Read Psalm 140)

††

What does the Bible verse or Bible chapter mean to you?

_____

_____

How do you most often express your love to others?

_____

_____

List your PRAYER REQUESTS and PRAY.

☐ _____

☐ _____

☐ _____

☐ _____

What is God teaching you or asking you to do?

_____

_____

Date: _____

Marriage

Then the Lᴏʀᴅ God said, "It is not good for the man to be alone.
I will make a helper who is just right for him."

(Genesis 2:18; Read Psalm 141)

††

What does the Bible verse or Bible chapter mean to you?

_____

_____

What makes a good marriage?

_____

_____

List your PRAYER REQUESTS and PRAY.

☐ _____

☐ _____

☐ _____

☐ _____

What is God teaching you or asking you to do?

_____

_____

Date: _____

Parents 1

Honor your father and mother. Then you will live a long, full life
in the land the LORD your God is giving you.

(Exodus 20:12; Read Psalm 142)

††

What does the Bible verse or Bible chapter mean to you?

_____

_____

How can you improve your relationship with your parents?

_____

_____

List your PRAYER REQUESTS and PRAY.

☐ _____

☐ _____

☐ _____

☐ _____

What is God teaching you or asking you to do?

_____

_____

Date: _____

Parents 2

And we know that God causes everything to work together
for the good of those who love God
and are called according to his purpose for them.

(Romans 8:28; Read Psalm 143)

††

What does the Bible verse or Bible chapter mean to you?

_____

_____

Name 2 ways you can show love to babies and small children.

_____

_____

List your PRAYER REQUESTS and PRAY.

- ☐ _____
- ☐ _____
- ☐ _____
- ☐ _____

What is God teaching you or asking you to do?

_____

_____

Date: _____

Widows

Take care of any widow who has no one else to care for her. But if she
has children or grandchildren, their first responsibility is to show
godliness at home and repay their parents by taking care of them.
This is something that pleases God.

(1 Timothy 5:3-4; Read Psalm 144)

††

What does the Bible verse or Bible chapter mean to you?

_____

_____

How can you show love to a widow this week?

_____

_____

List your PRAYER REQUESTS and PRAY.

☐ _____

☐ _____

☐ _____

☐ _____

What is God teaching you or asking you to do?

_____

_____

It's A Relationship

College Students holding Hands

"To who I can become and where I can reach
If I invest nothing less than my best in today.
For now, where I am may not be perfect
But what I have is enough to keep me going
If only I make the most and get
the best of each [day]."

Poetry Credit: *If Only*, Glory
C. Odemene ©2013

Date: _____

Abortion

The Lord said, "I knew you before I formed you in your
mother's womb. Before you were born I set you apart
and appointed you as my prophet to the nations."

(Jeremiah 1:5; Read Psalm 145)

††

What does the Bible verse or Bible chapter mean to you?

_____

_____

How does God view abortion? Do you think He forgives abortions?

_____

_____

List your PRAYER REQUESTS and PRAY.

☐ _____

☐ _____

☐ _____

☐ _____

What is God teaching you or asking you to do?

_____

_____

Date: _____

Abstinence

God's will is for you to be holy, so stay away from all sexual sin.
Then each of you will control his own body
and live in holiness and honor—

(1 Thessalonians 4:3-4; Read Psalm 146)

††

What does the Bible verse or Bible chapter mean to you?

_____

_____

How might abstinence before marriage protect a person?

_____

_____

List your PRAYER REQUESTS and PRAY.

☐ _____

☐ _____

☐ _____

☐ _____

What is God teaching you or asking you to do?

_____

_____

Date: _____

Conscience

Pray for us, for our conscience is clear and we want to live
honorably in everything we do.

(Hebrews 13:18; Read Psalm 147)

++

What does the Bible verse or Bible chapter mean to you?

_____

_____

Define <u>conscience</u>. Use a dictionary or digital device.

_____

_____

List your PRAYER REQUESTS and PRAY.

☐ _____

☐ _____

☐ _____

☐ _____

What is God teaching you or asking you to do?

_____

_____

Date: _____

Date Rape

The Lord is close to the broken-hearted;
he rescues those whose spirits are crushed.

(Psalm 34:18; Read Psalm 148)

††

What does the Bible verse or Bible chapter mean to you?

_____

_____

Read Deuteronomy 22:25-27 and explain it in your own words.

_____

_____

List your PRAYER REQUESTS and PRAY.

☐ _____

☐ _____

☐ _____

☐ _____

What is God teaching you or asking you to do?

_____

_____

Date: _____

Incest

You must never have sexual relations with
a close relative, for I am the LORD.

(Leviticus 18:6; Read Psalm 149)

††

What does the Bible verse or Bible chapter mean to you?

_____

_____

Why do you think God says incest is wrong?

_____

_____

List your PRAYER REQUESTS and PRAY.

☐ _____

☐ _____

☐ _____

☐ _____

What is God teaching you or asking you to do?

_____

_____

_____

Date: _____

Modesty

And I want women to be modest in their appearance. They should
wear decent and appropriate clothing and not draw attention to
themselves by the way they fix their hair or by wearing gold or pearls
or expensive clothes. For women who claim to be devoted to God
should make themselves attractive by the good things they do.

(1 Timothy 2:9-10; Read Psalm 150)

†††

What does the Bible verse or Bible chapter mean to you?

_____

_____

How does dressing modestly honor the Lord?

_____

_____

List your PRAYER REQUESTS and PRAY.

☐ _____

☐ _____

☐ _____

☐ _____

What is God teaching you or asking you to do?

_____

_____

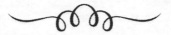

Date: _____

One Man ~ One Woman / Homosexuality

Do not practice homosexuality, having sex with another man
as with a woman. It is a detestable sin.

(Leviticus 18:22; Read Proverbs 1)

††

What does the Bible verse or Bible chapter mean to you?

_____

_____

How can you pray for someone in a homosexual lifestyle?

_____

_____

List your PRAYER REQUESTS and PRAY.

☐ _____

☐ _____

☐ _____

☐ _____

What is God teaching you or asking you to do?

_____

_____

Date: _____

Past Failures

No, dear brothers and sisters, I have not achieved it, but I focus on this one thing: Forgetting the past and looking forward to what lies ahead. I press on to reach the end of the race and receive the heavenly prize for which God, through Christ Jesus, is calling us.

(Philippians 3:13-14; Read Proverbs 2)

††

What does the Bible verse or Bible chapter mean to you?

_____

_____

How would you advise a friend to overcome the regret of a past sin?

_____

_____

List your PRAYER REQUESTS and PRAY.

☐ _____

☐ _____

☐ _____

☐ _____

What is God teaching you or asking you to do?

_____

_____

Date: _____

Purity

God's will is for you to be holy, so stay away from all sexual sin.
Then each of you will control his own body and live in
holiness and honor— not in lustful passion like the pagans
who do not know God and his ways.

(1 Thessalonians 4:3-5; Read Proverbs 3)

††

What does the Bible verse or Bible chapter mean to you?

_____

_____

Why should you make a decision for purity in all aspects of your life?

_____

_____

List your PRAYER REQUESTS and PRAY.

☐ _____

☐ _____

☐ _____

☐ _____

What is God teaching you or asking you to do?

_____

_____

Date: _____

Regrets

Have mercy on me, O God, because of your unfailing love.
Because of your great compassion, blot out the stain of my sins.
Wash me clean from my guilt. Purify me from my sin.
For I recognize my rebellion; it haunts me day and night.

(Psalm 51:1-3; Read Proverbs 4)

††

What does the Bible verse or Bible chapter mean to you?

_____

_____

What can our regrets teach us?

_____

_____

List your PRAYER REQUESTS and PRAY.

☐ _____

☐ _____

☐ _____

☐ _____

What is God teaching you or asking you to do?

_____

_____

Date: _____

Rejection

And I am convinced that nothing can ever separate us from God's
love. Neither death nor life, neither angels nor demons, neither
our fears for today nor our worries about tomorrow – not even
the powers of hell can separate us from God's love.

(Romans 8:38; Read Proverbs 5)

✝✝✝

What does the Bible verse or Bible chapter mean to you?

_____

_____

Describe how rejection can affect a person.

_____

_____

List your PRAYER REQUESTS and PRAY.

☐ _____

☐ _____

☐ _____

☐ _____

What is God teaching you or asking you to do?

_____

_____

Date: _____

Respect

Respect everyone, and love your Christian brothers and sisters.
Fear God, and respect the king.

(1 Peter 2:17; Read Proverb 6)

††

What does the Bible verse or Bible chapter mean to you?

_____

_____

Describe a person you really respect. Why do you respect them?

_____

_____

List your PRAYER REQUESTS and PRAY.

☐ _____

☐ _____

☐ _____

☐ _____

What is God teaching you or asking you to do?

_____

_____

Date: _____

Sexual Abuse

The LORD examines both the righteous and the wicked.
He hates those who love violence.

(Psalm 11:5; Read Proverbs 7)

††

What does the Bible verse or Bible chapter mean to you?

_____

_____

Why is "sexual abuse" considered a violent crime?

_____

_____

List your PRAYER REQUESTS and PRAY.

☐ _____

☐ _____

☐ _____

☐ _____

What is God teaching you or asking you to do?

_____

_____

Date: _____

Sexual Sin

"Brothers, listen! We are here to proclaim that through
this man Jesus there is forgiveness for your sins. Everyone
who believes in him is declared right with God
—something the law of Moses could never do."
Run from sexual sin! No other sin so clearly affects the body as this
one does. For sexual immorality is a sin against your own body.

(Acts 13:38-39; 1 Corinthians 6:18; Read Proverbs 8)

†††

What does the Bible verse or Bible chapter mean to you?

_____

_____

Name 2 reasons why sexual sin of any kind should be avoided.

_____

_____

List your PRAYER REQUESTS and PRAY.

☐ _____

☐ _____

☐ _____

☐ _____

What is God teaching you or asking you to do?

_____

_____

Date: _____

Sexually Transmitted Diseases (STD's)

Don't be misled—you cannot mock the justice of God. You
will always harvest what you plant. Those who live only
to satisfy their own sinful nature will harvest decay and
death from that sinful nature. But, those who live to please
the Spirit will harvest everlasting life from the Spirit.

(Galatians 6:7-8; Read Proverbs 9)

††

What does the Bible verse or Bible chapter mean to you?

_____

_____

How would abstinence alleviate our nation's STD problem?

_____

_____

List your PRAYER REQUESTS and PRAY.

- ☐ _____
- ☐ _____
- ☐ _____
- ☐ _____

What is God teaching you or asking you to do?

_____

_____

Date: _____

Unequally Yoked

Don't team up with those who are unbelievers. How can righteousness
be a partner with wickedness? How can light live with darkness?
How can a believer be a partner with an unbeliever?

(2 Corinthians 6:14, 15b; Read Proverbs 10)

†††

What does the Bible verse or Bible chapter mean to you?

_____

_____

Is it okay for a Christian to marry a non-Christian? Why or why not?

_____

_____

List your PRAYER REQUESTS and PRAY.

☐ _____

☐ _____

☐ _____

☐ _____

What is God teaching you or asking you to do?

_____

_____

Date: _____

Unplanned Pregnancy

Jesus said, "So don't worry at all about having enough food and clothing. Why be like the heathen? For they take pride in all these things and are deeply concerned about them. But your heavenly Father already knows perfectly well that you need them, and he will give them to you if you give him first place in your life and live as he wants you to. So don't be anxious about tomorrow...live one day at a time."

(Matthew 6:31-34 LB; Read Proverbs 11)

††

What does the Bible verse or Bible chapter mean to you?

_____

_____

How can God take care of a couple with an unplanned pregnancy?

_____

_____

List your PRAYER REQUESTS and PRAY.

☐ _____

☐ _____

☐ _____

☐ _____

What is God teaching you or asking you to do?

_____

_____

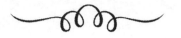

Date: _____

Virginity

Jesus said, "But 'God made them male and female' from the beginning of creation. This explains why a man leaves his father and mother and is joined to his wife, and the two are united into one. Since they are no longer two but one, let no one split apart what God has joined together."

(Mark 10:6-9; Read Proverbs 12)

††

What does the Bible verse or Bible chapter mean to you?

_____

_____

What is your opinion of teen chastity pledges?

_____

_____

List your PRAYER REQUESTS and PRAY.

☐ _____

☐ _____

☐ _____

☐ _____

What is God teaching you or asking you to do?

_____

_____

Date: _____

Youthful Lusts

Run from anything that stimulates youthful lusts. Instead,
pursue righteous living, faithfulness, love, and peace. Enjoy the
companionship of those who call on the Lord with pure hearts.

(2 Timothy 2:22; Read Proverbs 13)

++

What does the Bible verse or Bible chapter mean to you?

_____

_____

What are some ways you can avoid youthful lusts and live a pure life?

_____

_____

List your PRAYER REQUESTS and PRAY.

☐ _____

☐ _____

☐ _____

☐ _____

What is God teaching you or asking you to do?

_____

_____

It's The Way, The Truth, & The Life

Wooden Cross on a Decaying Wall

"Regardless of location and
condition, everyone
Who encountered Him,
testified: This is our God!
Yesterday, today or tomorrow, whatever I face
Rest my heart, my hope, my
gaze, on this our God."

Poetry Credit: *This is Our God,*
Glory C. Odemene ©2013

Date: _____

Eternal Life

For God so loved the world, that he gave his only begotten Son,
that whosoever believeth in him should not perish,
but have everlasting life. (Jesus to Nicodemus)

(John 3:16 KJV; Read Proverbs 14)

†††

What does the Bible verse or Bible chapter mean to you?

_____

_____

What are the consequences of not accepting Jesus?

_____

_____

List your PRAYER REQUESTS and PRAY.

☐ _____

☐ _____

☐ _____

☐ _____

What is God teaching you or asking you to do?

_____

_____

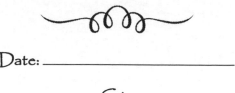

Date: _____

Sin

Do not let sin control the way you live; do not give in to sinful
desires. Do not let any part of your body become an instrument
of evil to serve sin. Instead, give yourselves completely to God,
for you were dead, but now you have new life. So use your whole
body as an instrument to do what is right for the glory of God.

(Romans 6:12-13; Read Proverbs 15)

††

What does the Bible verse or Bible chapter mean to you?

_____

_____

Define <u>sin</u>. Use a dictionary or digital device.

_____

_____

List your PRAYER REQUESTS and PRAY.

☐ _____

☐ _____

☐ _____

☐ _____

What is God teaching you or asking you to do?

_____

_____

Date: _____

Repentance

Peter replied, "Each of you must repent of your sins and turn to God, and be baptized in the name of Jesus Christ for the forgiveness of your sins. Then you will receive the gift of the Holy Spirit."

(Acts 2:38; Read Proverbs 16)

††

What does the Bible verse or Bible chapter mean to you?

_____

_____

Repentance is turning away from your sins. Are you willing to do that?

_____

_____

List your PRAYER REQUESTS and PRAY.

☐ _____

☐ _____

☐ _____

☐ _____

What is God teaching you or asking you to do?

_____

_____

Date: _____

Salvation

Jew and Gentile are the same in this respect.
They have the same Lord, who gives generously to all who call on him.
For "Everyone who calls on the name of the LORD will be saved."

(Romans 10:12-13; Read Proverbs 17)

✝✝

What does the Bible verse or Bible chapter mean to you?

_____

_____

Have you accepted Jesus Christ as your Savior? Why or why not?

_____

_____

List your PRAYER REQUESTS and PRAY.

☐ _____

☐ _____

☐ _____

☐ _____

What is God teaching you or asking you to do?

_____

_____

Date: _____

Jesus

Jesus told him, "I am the way, the truth, and the life.
No one can come to the Father except through me."

(John 14:6; Read Proverbs 18)

++

What does the Bible verse or Bible chapter mean to you?

_____

_____

What do you think holds some people back from accepting Christ?

_____

_____

List your PRAYER REQUESTS and PRAY.

- ☐ _____
- ☐ _____
- ☐ _____
- ☐ _____

What is God teaching you or asking you to do?

_____

_____

Date: _____

Grace

Sin is no longer your master, for you no longer live under
the requirements of the law. Instead, you live
under the freedom of God's grace.

(Romans 6:14; Read Proverbs 19)

††

What does the Bible verse or Bible chapter mean to you?

_____

_____

Define <u>grace</u>. Use a dictionary or digital device.

_____

_____

List your PRAYER REQUESTS and PRAY.

☐ _____

☐ _____

☐ _____

☐ _____

What is God teaching you or asking you to do?

_____

_____

Date: _____

Death

We all come to the end of our lives as naked and empty-handed
as on the day we were born. We can't take our riches with us.

(Ecclesiastes 5:15; Read Proverbs 20)

††

What does the Bible verse or Bible chapter mean to you?

_____

_____

Are you fearful of someone close to you (or yourself) dying? Explain.

_____

_____

List your PRAYER REQUESTS and PRAY.

- ☐ _____
- ☐ _____
- ☐ _____
- ☐ _____

What is God teaching you or asking you to do?

_____

_____

Date: _____

Eternal Security

Jesus said, "There is more than enough room in my Father's home. If this were not so, would I have told you that I am going to prepare a place for you? When everything is ready, I will come and get you, so that you will always be with me where I am.

(John 14:2-3; Read Proverbs 21)

††

What does the Bible verse or Bible chapter mean to you?

_____

_____

Why is accepting Jesus Christ important?

_____

_____

List your PRAYER REQUESTS and PRAY.

- ☐ _____
- ☐ _____
- ☐ _____
- ☐ _____

What is God teaching you or asking you to do?

_____

_____

Date: _____

Heaven

For we know that when this earthly tent we live in is taken down
(that is, when we die and leave this earthly body), we will have
a house in heaven, an eternal body made for us by
God himself and not by human hands.

(2 Corinthians 5:1; Read Proverbs 22)

††

What does the Bible verse or Bible chapter mean to you?

_____

_____

How do we know if we are going to heaven? Read John 3:16.

_____

_____

List your PRAYER REQUESTS and PRAY.

☐ _____

☐ _____

☐ _____

☐ _____

What is God teaching you or asking you to do?

_____

_____

It's Your Life

Man in a Wheelchair

"I choose to embrace life and just live it!
To stretch beyond the safety of familiar
Take what comes and make the most of it."

Poetry Credit: *Dare*, Glory
C. Odemene ©2014

Date: _____

Love

Love is patient and kind. Love is not jealous or boastful or
proud or rude. It does not demand its own way. It is not irritable,
and it keeps no record of being wronged. It does not rejoice
about injustice but rejoices whenever the truth wins out.

(1 Corinthians 13:4-6; Read Proverbs 23)

✝✝

What does the Bible verse or Bible chapter mean to you?

_____

_____

Name 2 characteristics of love from the verse above.

_____

_____

List your PRAYER REQUESTS and PRAY.

☐ _____

☐ _____

☐ _____

☐ _____

What is God teaching you or asking you to do?

_____

_____

Date: _____

Joy

Always be full of joy in the Lord. I say it again—rejoice!
Let everyone see that you are considerate in all you do.
Remember, the Lord is coming soon.

(Philippians 4:4-5; Read Proverbs 24)

✝✝✝

What does the Bible verse or Bible chapter mean to you?

_____

_____

Describe a joyful experience you have had with the Lord.

_____

_____

List your PRAYER REQUESTS and PRAY.

☐ _____

☐ _____

☐ _____

☐ _____

What is God teaching you or asking you to do?

_____

_____

Date: _____

Peace

Therefore, since we have been made right in God's sight by faith,
we have peace with God because of what
Jesus Christ our Lord has done for us.

(Romans 5:1; Read Proverbs 25)

††

What does the Bible verse or Bible chapter mean to you?

_____

_____

Have you ever prayed for peace? Explain why.

_____

_____

List your PRAYER REQUESTS and PRAY.

☐ _____

☐ _____

☐ _____

☐ _____

What is God teaching you or asking you to do?

_____

_____

Date: _____

Patience

Better to be patient than powerful;
better to have self-control than to conquer a city.

(Proverbs 16:32; Read Proverbs 26)

††

What does the Bible verse or Bible chapter mean to you?

_____

_____

How can you be more patient with others?

_____

_____

List your PRAYER REQUESTS and PRAY.

☐ _____

☐ _____

☐ _____

☐ _____

What is God teaching you or asking you to do?

_____

_____

Date: _____

Kindness

Get rid of all bitterness, rage, anger, harsh words, and
slander, as well as all types of evil behavior.
Instead, be kind to each other, tenderhearted, forgiving one
another, just as God through Christ has forgiven you.

(Ephesians 4:31-32; Read Proverbs 27)

††

What does the Bible verse or Bible chapter mean to you?

_____

_____

Have you ever experienced a kindness you didn't deserve? Explain it.

_____

_____

List your PRAYER REQUESTS and PRAY.

☐ _____

☐ _____

☐ _____

☐ _____

What is God teaching you or asking you to do?

_____

_____

Date: _____

Goodness

For the Kingdom of God is not a matter of what we eat or drink, but of living a life of goodness and peace and joy in the Holy Spirit.

(Romans 14:17; Read Proverbs 28)

††

What does the Bible verse or Bible chapter mean to you?

_____

_____

What does "living a life of goodness" look like?

_____

_____

List your PRAYER REQUESTS and PRAY.

☐ _____

☐ _____

☐ _____

☐ _____

What is God teaching you or asking you to do?

_____

_____

Date: _____

Faithfulness

Then Jesus said to the disciples, "Have faith in God. I tell you the truth, you can say to this mountain, 'May you be lifted up and thrown into the sea,' and it will happen and have no doubt in your heart."

(Mark 11:22-23; Read Proverbs 29)

††

What does the Bible verse or Bible chapter mean to you?

_____

_____

Describe a time you have felt uncomfortable sharing your beliefs.

_____

_____

List your PRAYER REQUESTS and PRAY.

☐ _____

☐ _____

☐ _____

☐ _____

What is God teaching you or asking you to do?

_____

_____

Date: _____

Gentleness

Let your gentleness be evident to all. The Lord is near.

(Philippians 4:5 NIV; Read Proverbs 30)

✝✝✝

What does the Bible verse or Bible chapter mean to you?

_____

_____

Why do you think a gentle answer deflects anger?

_____

_____

List your PRAYER REQUESTS and PRAY.

☐ _____

☐ _____

☐ _____

☐ _____

What is God teaching you or asking you to do?

_____

_____

Date: _____

Self-Control

So think clearly and exercise self-control.
Look forward to the gracious salvation that will
come to you when Jesus Christ is revealed to the world.

(1 Peter 1:13; Read Proverbs 31)

††

What does the Bible verse or Bible chapter mean to you?

_____

_____

How does reading God's Word help you to be more self-controlled?

_____

_____

List your PRAYER REQUESTS and PRAY.

☐ _____

☐ _____

☐ _____

☐ _____

What is God teaching you or asking you to do?

_____

_____

Appendix:
Have You Heard of the
Four Spiritual Laws?

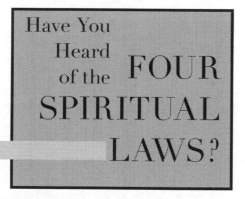

Just as there are physical laws that govern
the physical universe, so are there spiritual laws
that govern your relationship with God.

Law 1

God loves you and offers a wonderful plan for your life.

God's Love

"God so loved the world that He gave His one and
only Son, that whoever believes in Him shall not
perish but have eternal life" (John 3:16, NIV)

God's Plan

[Christ speaking] "I came that they might have life, and might have it
abundantly"
[that it might be full and meaningful] (John 10:10).

Why is it that most people are not experiencing that abundant life?

Because ...

Law 2

**Man is sinful and separated from God.
Therefore, he cannot know and experience
God's love and plan for his life.**

Man is Sinful

"All have sinned and fall short of the glory of God" (Romans 3:23)

Man was created to have fellowship with God; but, because of
his own stubborn self-will, he chose to go his own independent
way and fellowship with God was broken. This self-will,
characterized by an attitude of active rebellion or passive
indifference, is an evidence of what the Bible calls sin.

Man is separated

"The wages of sin is death" [spiritual separation from God] (Romans 6:23)

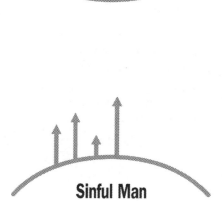

Holy God

Sinful Man

This diagram illustrates that
God is holy and man is sinful.
A great gulf separates the two.
The arrows illustrate that man is
continually trying to reach God
and the abundant life through his
own efforts, such as a good life,
philosophy, or religion
-but he inevitably fails.

The third law explains the only
way to bridge this gulf ...

Law 3

**Jesus Christ is God's only provision for man's sin.
Through Him you can know and experience
God's love and plan for your life.**

He died in Our Place

"God demonstrates His own love toward us, in that while we were yet
sinners, Christ died for us"
(Romans 5:8)

He Rose from the Dead

"Christ died for our sins ... He was buried ... He was raised on the third day,
according to the Scriptures ... He appeared to Peter, then to the twelve.
After that He appeared to more than five hundred..."
(1 Corinthians 15:3-6)

He Is the Only Way to God

"Jesus said to him, 'I am the way, and the truth, and the life, no one
comes to the Father but through Me'"
(John 14:6)

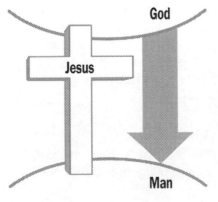

This diagram illustrates that
God has bridged the gulf that
separates us from Him by
sending His Son, Jesus Christ,
to die on the cross in our place
to pay the penalty for our sins.

It is not enough just to
know these three laws ...

200

Law 4

We must individually receive Jesus Christ as Savior and Lord; then we can know and experience God's love and plan for our lives.

We Must Receive Christ

"As many as received Him, to them He gave the right to become children of God, even to those who believe in His name"
(John 1:12)

We receive Christ through faith

"By grace you have been saved through faith; and that not of yourselves, it is the gift of God; not as result of works that no one should boast"
(Ephesians 2:8,9)

When We Receive Christ, We Experience a New Birth
(Read John 3:1-8)

We Receive Christ through Personal Invitation

[Christ speaking] "Behold, I stand at the door and knock; if any one hears My voice and opens the door, I will come in to him"
(Revelation 3:20)

Receiving Christ involves turning to God from self (repentance) and trusting Christ to come into our lives to forgive our sins and to make us what He wants us to be. Just to agree **intellectually** that Jesus Christ is the Son of God and that He died on the cross for our sins is not enough.
Nor is it enough to have an
emotional experience.
We receive Jesus Christ by **faith**, as an act of the **will**.

These two circles represent two kinds of lives:

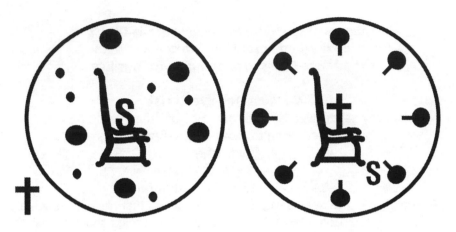

Self-Directed Life

S-Self is on the throne

✝-Christ is outside the life

●-Interests are directed
by self, often resulting in
discord and frustration

Christ-Directed Life

✝-Christ is in the life
and on the throne

S-Self is yielding to Christ,
resulting in harmony
with God's plan

●-Interests are directed
by Christ, resulting in
harmony with God's plan

Which circle best represents your life?

Which circle would you like to have represent your life?

The following explains how you can receive Christ

You Can Receive Christ Right Now by Faith Through Prayer
(Prayer is talking with God)

God knows your heart and is not so concerned with your words as He is with the attitude of your heart. The following is a suggested prayer:

> Lord Jesus, I need You. Thank You for dying on the cross for my sins. I open the door of my life and receive You as my Savior and Lord. Thank You for forgiving my sins and giving me eternal life. Take control of the throne of my life. Make me the kind of person You want me to be.

Does this prayer express the desire of your heart?
If it does, I invite you to pray this prayer right now, and
Christ will come into your life, as He promised.

Leader/Facilitator Guide

The purpose of this guide is to explain the mechanics and structure of *Anchor Me: Laying a Foundation in Bible Study and Prayer* and to give you suggestions for how to best utilize this workbook with your particular group.

I am so excited to be able to bring you *Anchor Me* for your large or small group study. My prayer is that your participants will grow in their desire for daily Bible study and increase their dependency on the Lord for the needs in their lives through prayer. My goal is to encourage your group to develop a consistency in their devotional time by including Bible study and prayer so they can become all that the Lord wants them to be.

For purposes of this guide, I have used the following words to represent certain entities:

Leader:	Main *Adult Leader* of the entire group
Meeting:	The entire time spent at host facility
Facilitator:	*Leader* of a small group
Colleagues:	*Friends* who work beside each other to fulfill God's purpose for the group
Participants/Group:	Those who attend the sessions
Age Range:	Varies
Session:	Your small group meeting
Anchor Me	Sometimes called a devotional, journal, prayer journal, or workbook.

I. General Meeting Tips

A. Have materials approved by person(s) in authority.

B. Decide on a start date, end date, and time for your meetings. Adjust for holidays or special school conflicts.

C. Prepare maps for the directions to the host facility.

D. Decide whether refreshments will be served.

E. If you are planning to have a group contact list, ask the participants (or parents of young participants) if it is permissible for them to be put on a distribution list that will be given to the leader, facilitators, and participants. Tell them what will be included in the contact list: i.e. name, address, phone number, and email address.

F. Decide on the participant's cost for all books and supplies used. In most cases, if a participant pays for even a small portion of their materials, they feel a sense of ownership for the products.

G. Estimate the number of participants in your meeting, and order the books 4-6 weeks before your first session.

H. If applicable, promote the session through your church calendar, church newsletter, church bulletin, Bible study groups, calls, word of mouth, flyers, and social media.

I. Pray for your colleagues.

II. Leader and Facilitator Information

A. *Anchor Me* can be used as a devotional prayer journal for anyone that loves or works with people seeking to learn more about the Lord, like: grandparents, relatives, guardians, teachers, ministers, and Bible study leaders. It will help familiarize them with the relevant issues facing our culture today.

B. Using a copy of *Anchor Me*, the leader and facilitators should familiarize themselves with the structure of the book beforehand. Look through the *Table of Contents, List of Illustrations, Books of the Bible, Four Spiritual Laws, Leader/Facilitator Guide, Index*, and the *Notes* section. Also, read through the *Preface* and *Introduction* carefully in preparation for sharing with the group.

C. Work through at least one week of daily devotionals before the start date of your meetings. Be sure to complete each daily devotional and read the suggested Bible chapter. When the entire workbook is completed, you and your group will have read the entire books of Psalms and Proverbs.

D. Decide whether this devotional prayer journal will be used as the full focus of your meetings or as a supplement for a small group session. Small groups can foster friendships, accountability, and an ability to discuss issues in a smaller, more secure atmosphere, especially when there are a large number of participants in any one session.

E. Decide whether you will go through the book in order, through all eleven chapter topics, or whether you will select chapters according to the needs of the group. Sometimes a particular group might need to start at a place other than the first section. The pages are undated to allow for this freedom of movement and choice. Use your discernment and wisdom on how best to proceed with your group.

F. Set a time limit for your *Anchor Me* sessions. You might wish to begin with forty-five minutes for a large group session, or twenty minutes with a main lesson to start or follow the breakout sessions. The main leader could choose one of the daily topics to be the main topic of the day.

G. Decide if you will have adult facilitators or student facilitators leading the small group sessions. If you use student facilitators, you might consider a special training meeting for them.

H. If your group will be breaking up into smaller sessions, be sure the rooms or areas are clean and inviting, the thermostat is functioning at a comfortable temperature, and the lighting is adequate. In addition, have pens, pencils, paper, extra Bibles, and tissues available. The larger meeting room can serve as one of the break-off areas. Recognize that some people might have pet allergies or a fear of animals, so keeping pets confined would be a wise idea.

I. The leader should consider leading the *Anchor Me* session discussions the first few times before breaking up into smaller groups, as an example for the other facilitators to follow.

J. Open each session with a prayer.

K. As participants are led by the Holy Spirit, some may be convicted to make a decision for Christ. The leader and facilitators should be prepared to guide them in this very important decision. The leader and facilitator should familiarize themselves with CRU's (formerly Campus Crusade for Christ) *Have you heard of the Four Spiritual Laws?* It is located in the appendix of this book. This can be read to an individual or discussed with the group at some point.

Notes

III. Introductory Session with Leader, Facilitators, and Participants

A. Share the following information with the group:

1. Leader should communicate their expectations to the group at the first meeting.

2. Remind the participants that the purpose of these sessions is not to gossip, or focus on the negative, but to work on solutions that are Biblically based. Therefore, the majority of the conversation should dwell on what God says about the issues and principles the participants can use in their daily lives.

3. Remind the participants that much of what may be said in these sessions may be sensitive information, and that absolute confidentiality must be maintained. Therefore no recording on electronic devices or photographing should be permitted. Advise the group that if there is a sensitive issue that they would like to discuss, they can share it with a facilitator after the session concludes.

4. Discuss the use of appropriate language at all meetings.

5. Remind the participants that because the time is limited that they should try to keep their comments brief and to the point, to allow everyone to have a chance to speak.

6. Discuss that phones should be kept on silent and not answered throughout the session. Texting should also be delayed until the end of the meeting.

7. Leave the meeting place in order. The church staff or host's home will really appreciate it.

8. Distribute all materials and collect any payments required for materials, if applicable.

9. Confirm that all in the group have a Bible to accompany them in their study.

B. Discuss the set up and structure of *Anchor Me*.

1. Discuss the value of Bible study and prayer.

2. Discuss that prayer journaling is keeping track of one's prayer requests and answers. In *Anchor Me* there is a section to write your prayers down daily.

3. Discuss that this daily devotional prayer journal consists of 181 entries. You may want to include some discussion questions, such as what are the benefits of a daily, habitual Bible study and prayer time? In addition, discuss that the goal of these sessions is for them to discover what the Bible says about everyday issues facing the participants from a Biblical perspective.

4. The workbook pages usually take about 15 minutes to finish, excluding their prayer time since that can vary per person.

5. Remind the group that there is no right or wrong way to use this devotional prayer journal. They can write in the margins; they can continue their thoughts on the "Notes" pages, or leave some lines blank. There are no perfect answers for their personal journal.

6. Participants should be told that their copy of *Anchor Me* is a personal diary of their walk with the Lord. They should never feel obligated or pressured to share their innermost thoughts with the group. Individual group

members should only share what they feel comfortable sharing.

7. Discuss the entries included on the daily pages of *Anchor Me*, preferably with the participants viewing their copy or some copy of the book:

   a. An undated dateline
   b. A topic of interest
   c. A corresponding Bible verse
   d. A suggested chapter reading from either Psalms or Proverbs
   e. A "What does the Bible verse or Bible chapter mean to you?" section
   f. A thought provoking question for you to answer
   g. An area to write prayers requests and notes
   h. A "What is God teaching you or asking you to do?" section

IV. Before Session Facilitator Tips

A. Work in your personal copy of *Anchor Me* each day on the pages your group will be reviewing during the upcoming session.

B. Ask the Lord to give you a loving spirit towards each person coming to your group.

C. Pray for the participants in your group by name, along with any special prayer requests they may have given you to pray for.

D. Ask God to give you wisdom and guidance as you lead your group in a manner glorifying to the Lord Jesus Christ.

E. Mark areas of discussion and have a plan in place for facilitating a discussion. Sample questions to ask your group could be the following:

1. "Does anyone have a praise report that you would like to share?"

2. "How did God use your devotional time with Him this week?"

3. "Would anyone like to share what the Bible verse meant on page _?"

4. "Does anyone have an answer to the question on page _ on the topic of ___?"

5. You can go page by page, asking all or just a few questions from each page, depending on your time.

6. Find other related Bible verses on the topics to share with your participants.

7. Remember that as a facilitator, your role is to guide and discuss the topics and Bible verses with the group. If you have not been a facilitator before, you may want to take some time to research how to lead your group to function properly.

V. During Session Facilitator Tips

A. Begin and end on time. If this is difficult for you, ask someone to be your personal clock-keeper and help you to keep an eye on the time.

B. Remind the participants of group confidentiality and that not everything is wise to share in the group study, i.e. your best friend is pregnant.

C. Remind your participants that Bible study and prayer is beneficial to them—to increase their faith, to give them spiritual guidance, and to learn God's will.

D. Be kindhearted and compassionate.

E. Be prepared if you need to redirect or stop a conversation if it is becoming too personal or not suited for the discussion at hand. This would be a good topic to discuss with the other group leaders before the sessions start.

F. Expect that you might encounter the need to make some adjustments in how you lead your group. Adjustments may be needed due to the dynamics of your group, the age of the participants, or the nature of the topics.

G. Allow for silence sometimes when a question is asked. This might be the catalyst for a shy person to speak up. A shy person might speak up if you prompt the participants by saying, "Let's hear from someone who hasn't spoken yet."

H. Occasionally, you might want to remind participants of the group rules, especially if you have new participants arrive.

I.   By all means, if you are creative, use your God-given creativity to lead a discussion.

J.   If there is time left at the end of your session, have someone read the Psalms or Proverbs chapter listed aloud.

After Session Facilitator Tips

A. Pray for the specific needs of your participants.

B. Pray for next week's session and for the Holy Spirit to draw new members to come to your meetings.

C. Follow up on any important issues. If you've promised to pray for someone or provide them some information, be sure to make yourself a note so you can follow through.

D. Pray for your colleagues.

E. Prepare for next week's session.

Notes

Index

Notes

Notes

Notes

Notes

Notes

Notes

Notes

I would greatly appreciate it if you would take a little bit of your time to leave a review on Amazon or other book review sites. Reviews are hard to come by, but they help so much in getting the word out to potential readers who may desire to learn more about foundations in Bible Study and Prayer. Thank you so much.

Patti Greene

Books by Patti Greene

Anchor Me: Laying a Foundation in Bible Study and Prayer
ISBN: 978-1-4908-9317-4 (sc)
ISBN: 978-1-4908-9531-4 (e)

Awaken Me: Growing Deeper in Bible Study and Prayer
ISBN: 978-1-4908-9318-1 (sc)
ISBN: 978-1-4908-9320-4 (hc)
ISBN: 978-1-4908-9319-8 (e)